WHAT OTHERS ARE SAYING...

Youth Ministry as we have known it for the past fifty years is in trouble. A shifting culture and a better understanding of the role families must play in discipleship are changing everything. The Greenhouse Project makes a significant contribution to the conversation about where youth ministry needs to go from here.

Dr. Jimmy Scroggins
Pastor 1st Baptist Church
West Palm Beach, Florida

The Greenhouse Project provides a much needed biblical view of ministry from some of today's leading voices for student ministry. This healthy approach will better equip you to enlist, equip and engage this generation for the cause of Christ.

Brent Crowe
Executive Director
Student Leadership University

I have read many books on youth ministry that are excellent and some I will actually recommend. *The Greenhouse Project* will be in the top five that I encourage those who love teenagers to read. It is one of the few youth ministry books that actually gives thought to helping youth ministers develop a plan for equipping students in dealing with current pressures and those that will come to them in the future. Calhoun's quote, "You cannot lose what you never truly had" lends credence to his recommendation that we "tell the truth about the cost of discipleship." "Enlist, Equip, Engage" will be a practical aid to those who love students, parents, and youth work

Dr. Johnny Derouen
Professor of Student Minist
Southwestern Theological S

While so many today are quick to demand a new way of doing things, you will find this book refreshingly practical and profoundly deep at the same time. Written by veterans who have lived through multiple "latest trends," they look beyond the clever and capture the clear truth of life-on-life transformation. I highly encourage you to capture the practical wisdom this book provides...you will be a better leader for it. In the end the whole body of Christ may stand and exclaim together, "We will tell the next generation the praiseworthy deeds of the Lord, his power and the wonders he has done." (Psalm 78:4)

Dr. Dann Spader
Founder & Director of SonLife Ministries

I trust Mike Calhoun the man – his thoughts, his methods, and his concerns. And I've experienced Mike Calhoun the leader – uniquely blend orthodoxy with orthopraxy packaging it in a way that's easy to the eyes and challenging to the soul.

Dr. Kary Oberbrunner
"Recovering Pharisee," **author of The Fine Line and founder of Redeem the Day Ministries**

Once again, Mike and Mel have produced a tool that is a must for every youth pastor, Ed guy and pastor. It hits on the value of what is most important in Youth Ministry: the Word, parents, family, discipleship, biblical worldview and truth. With a plan to enlist, equip, and engage this generation to be all that God desires them to be. In addition to the wisdom from those who have walked with teenagers, parents and the local church for decades, Mike and Mel have recruited some of the most incredible leaders to share in this project. Again, it's must reading, so pick up a copy or start this copy today.

Phil Newberry, Student Pastor
Bellevue Baptist Church, Memphis, TN

The Greenhouse Project because it takes the whole concept of youth ministry to a new level. Pastors, youth leaders, parents and all who care about the next will generation will welcome this book and learn from it. I strongly encourage anyone who wants a 21st-century youth ministry that is both contemporary and biblical to read *The Greenhouse Project*. It is life changing!

Dr. Ray Pritchard
President, Keep Believing Ministries
Author: Stealth Attack, The Healing Power of Forgiveness,
Man of Honor

Parents and youth leaders need practical steps in order to launch young people into the fields of influence. Mike and Mel have given us an invaluable resource that every parent and youth leader needs in their tool box.

Dr. Troy W. Temple, Assistant Professor of Youth Ministry
The Southern Baptist Theological Seminary
Associate Director, The International Center for Youth &
Family Ministry,
Louisville, KY

With *The Greenhouse Project*, Mike and Mel have put their fingers on the pulse of a perennial question that every youth pastor must answer for their own ministry – "What is our strategy for identifying, training, and releasing students for missional leadership RIGHT NOW?" This book is biblically-grounded, philosophically-principled, and practically-oriented. As a youth pastor, I am excited to finally have a resource on this subject that is worth recommending.

Brandon Shields
High School Pastor
Highview Baptist Church

I fear that many of us in youth ministry are consumed with "doing" without first "asking." Consequently, we lose (or never have) a clear sense of purpose and direction. *The Greenhouse Project* not only asks the difficult questions that need to be asked, but goes on to offer solid, biblically-based advice that I believe will bear great fruit in the spiritual growth of students. . . both now and into their adult years. I recommend that all youth workers seriously and prayerfully wrestle with this book.

Dr. Walt Mueller
Center for Parent/Youth Understanding

There has never been a time when the need for godly Christian leaders has been greater. We know that the best way to find them is to train them up when they are young. I know that because Mike Calhoun is an example as a young person once involved in our ministry. What Mike learned as a young person has stayed with him and he has multiplied it thousands of times throughout his life. We must all leverage our resources to accomplish the continuation of this line of godly leaders. I commend Mike and this project for tackling this strategic task.

Paul Fleischmann, President
National Network of Youth Ministries

What a great picture! We all need to visualize the "perfect environment for growth" as we lead and teach students. The Greenhouse Project paints that picture.

Randy Hall
rhall@studentlife.net

The words of this book are not theory but wisdom from those who have labored faithfully and who have great "sweat equity" in student ministry!

Steve Wright
Student Pastor and author of the book, Rethink

MIKE CALHOUN & MEL WALKER

Cultivating Students of Influence

THE GREENHOUSE PROJECT
Cultivating Students of Influence

Copyright © 2009 by Mike Calhoun and Mel Walker
Published by Word of Life Fellowship, Inc.
P.O. Box 600
Schroon Lake, Ny 12870
www.wol.org

Unless otherwise noted, all scripture quotations are taken from the New King James Version Bible® (NKJV). Copyright © 1979, 1980, 1982, Thomas Nelson Inc., Publishers. Used by permission.

Scripture quotations marked (NIV) are taken from the Holy Bible, New International Version®. Copyright © 1973, 1978, 1984. Used by permission of Zondervan.

Scripture quotations marked (NASB95) are taken from the New American Standard Bible®. Copyright © 1995 by The Lockman Foundation. Used by permission.

Scripture quotations marked (KJV) are taken from the Holy Bible, Kings James Version.

Please note: The authors have prepared a STUDENT GUIDE to accompany this text. An explanation of the guide is found in the back of this book.

Cover design by Boire Design
ISBN: 978-1-935475-00-2
www.greenhouseproject.wol.org

Printed in the United States of America

printed on 10% post-consumer recycled paper

ACKNOWLEDGEMENTS

Books are a collaborative effort combining a dream, hard work and belief. This book has been a dream of ours for several years. Many people, including the contributing writers, editors, proof readers and the Word of Life curriculum production team have spent many long hours working to make this book a possibility; however, you still need someone to believe in the concept who is willing to publish the book.

We want to express our sincere thanks to Dr. Joe Jordan, the Executive Director of Word of Life Fellowship, for believing in this project. The philosophy communicated in the next sixteen chapters is a snapshot of the commitment Joe and the ministry of Word of Life have lived for many years. His enthusiastic endorsement and support has enabled us to fulfill this dream.

We are grateful to Joe and the Word of Life ministry for saying yes to this project and being the vehicle for publishing The Greenhouse Project – Cultivating Students of Influence.

Mike and Mel

:=

TABLE OF CONTENTS

INTRODUCTION

The basic purpose of a greenhouse is to prepare plants for life outside of the greenhouse. Plants are given food, water, sunshine, and heat to grow enough so that they can survive and thrive outside of that environment. We realize that like any analogy, our comparison between church student ministry and greenhouses will undoubtedly break down somewhere along the line, but, the basic illustration is sound. The greenhouse is not the end result. It is a place of growth and maturity. It is a place of safety and security. The ultimate objective of a greenhouse is for the plants to make it outside. Life outside is the goal. A lifetime of strength and maturity should be the result.

Certainly we can visualize the parallel here. Our churches, partnering with Godly parents, can feed students through a careful, complete, and creative study of God's Word. We can provide balanced, life-related activities and functions to demonstrate the relationship between biblical principles and real life. We can also provide them with models of how to live for the Lord in the form of consistent and Christlike adults.

Our ultimate focus, however, must be for our students to grow up and continue living for God as adults. The very nature of student ministry is that it is a terminal program. There's an ending point. Perhaps it is cultural to a point, but most student ministries end when our students graduate from high school. Many student ministries provide lessons and activities for adolescents (that's what we do – we're student workers, we work with student) and then once they leave high school - we make them leave the safety and security of our student groups to forge their own way into the world of adulthood.

So, the key question, of course, is this. Are they ready? Are our kids mature enough in their faith and in their own personal walk with God to go on living for God once they leave the home and student group?

That's the crux of the issue that we want to address in The Greenhouse Project – Cultivating Students of Influence. We went on a search for answers and success stories. We identified this list of writers from a variety of backgrounds, but with a common commitment for cultivating the growth of students in their relationship with God. In this anthology we've gathered the collective wisdom of some of the best voices in today's student ministry from all across the country.

These people are specialists and experts in their own disciplines. They each are genuine practitioners. All have proven track records of success in developing student leaders. But, they also share another commonality – they each are absolutely committed to the life-shaping nutrients of Scripture. Each writer identified in this book would heartily "amen" the foundational truth of Biblical passages such as 2 Timothy 3:16 and 17, " All Scripture is given by inspiration of God, and is profitable for doctrine, for reproof, for correction, for instruction in righteousness, that the man of God may be complete, thoroughly equipped for every good work."

This is our grand task as student workers, to cultivate students to be mature – to be "thoroughly equipped" for what God has for them in the future. This is why our greenhouse analogy works. We must focus on the fact that we are preparing our students for life outside of student group. Our students will grow up - and our goal must be to help them grow spiritually.

We want them to become leaders and influencers of others. We are more than baby sitters – just watching over the baby plants until they leave the greenhouse to live or die on their own. Student ministry is much, much more than that. We must be very intentional about the cultivating process so that when our students leave the controlled environment of the home and student group they are ready to handle it. If we're doing our job well – we should see student-after-student experience the success of going on for God as adults.

Perhaps you question why we used the word "project" in the title of this book. It is not because we see students as experiments but rather that the word implies intention and purpose. It signifies that we must organize the factors inside the greenhouse to mesh together in a single focus with a measurable, desired result. The Apostle Paul used this same basic illustration in 1 Corinthians 3:6 and 7, "I planted, Apollos watered, but God gave the increase. So then neither he who plants nor he who waters is anything, but God who gives the increase." Each parent and adult student worker has his or her own role and responsibility in God's great work but the ultimate growth is up to God. We each intentionally do our parts to help students grow in Christ – the increase or growth is up to Him.

So we ask you to read this book with a heart for growth and a passionate desire to help students go on for God as adults. Our prayer is that YOUR greenhouse project will indeed cultivate students of influence into growing, maturing student leaders.

Mike and Mel

THE GREENHOUSE PROJECT: Cultivating Students of Influence

CHAPTER 1

Beyond the Status Quo:
Defining Student Leadership

I always thought that greenhouses were just places where you protected plants until I visited some greenhouses owned by a friend of mine in Florida. I had assumed they were emergency hospitals, not birthing rooms. I had envisioned people checking in their plants so they could be revived or patched up and then given back until the process needed to be repeated.

Unfortunately, I think this has become our perspective about church youth ministries. Students are checked in with the youth doctors (by this, I mean leaders) with the hope that by the time they are picked up, they have been fixed. Christian homes are often viewed in a similar fashion. We reason that if we can just keep them protected from evil so they don't do anything really bad, then we have done our job.

But greenhouses are more than hospitals or isolation chambers. Greenhouses are places of nurturing, strengthening, and preparing these tender plants we call *students* for a productive life. There are some critical care duties performed in greenhouses and they are also places of protection, but all this is done with the idea of preparing the plants to leave, grow, and reproduce.

Our churches and our families must work together with a unified biblical strategy to cultivate students of influence. The teen years are not a "holding pattern," but should be a time of utilizing the power of youth. We are not preparing them to be leaders in the future; we are preparing them now for this moment. Being salt and light is not a post-graduate concept.

Being salt and light is not a post-graduate concept.

There has been a great deal of discussion and debate over the mass exodus of students from the church following high school. Recently, I was discussing this with a group of youth pastors and I made the statement, "You cannot lose what you never truly had." Many of those whom we say we are losing were never committed or connected; they just attended.

In an interview with Center for Parent/Youth Understanding (CPYU), Tim Clydesdale, author of *The First Year Out: Understanding American Teens After High School*, said, "Those who "walked away" from their faith during college made the decision to do so long before their college years—they just waited for the freedom of college to enact that choice." He goes on to say, "Sadly, most youth ministries are long on fun and fluff and short on listening and thoughtful engagement. The former produces a million paper boats; the latter produces a handful of seaworthy ships." [1] In order to change this, we must have a plan to equip students to deal with current pressures and pressures to come in the future.

This will not take place in emergency youth hospitals and isolation chambers; it will take place in the trenches. It seems that many of the articles on student ministry are addressing the failure to stabilize students but only a few are addressing the answer. There appears to be some consensus (at least in print) as to the way to change the paradigm of youth ministry. Now we need to make a commitment to transfer these changes from the printed page to life's arena.

Some of the basic ideas for this process should not be new to us as they arise from long-standing biblical mandates. But perhaps our ministries have been program-driven so long that these ideas appear to be revolutionary. They definitely will be if we make the commitment to implement them at any cost.

BIG PICTURE MINISTRY

* Reaching students with the Gospel and cultivating them into genuine disciples.

* Teaching students the current "hot topics" while simultaneously rooting them in biblical doctrine and principles.

* Having multiple adults involved in a student's life with true life-on-life ministry. This means youth leaders and parents working together.

* Teaching students to feed themselves spiritually, with the realization that it is a personal responsibility.

* Having some form of accountability for every student. This is not a legalistic checklist that will make them spiritual or keep them from evil, but it is a way of helping them navigate through the minefield of life.

Recently, I was with a group of youth pastors for a brainstorming session concerning student ministry. They were divided into four small groups and the question was asked, "What do you think the top ten goals of youth ministry should be?" After lengthy and lively discussions in all four groups, they shared their decisions. Here are the lists of two of the groups.

Group 1

* All students reading the Bible every day
* Honesty with God in prayer
* Students honoring God
* Students being godly leaders who impact their world
* Students proactively sharing their faith
* Students being moved to a ministry mindset of servanthood
* Students being equipped to share the Gospel
* Establishing accountability in a personal small group

Group 2:

* Students sharing the Gospel
* Clear partnership with parents
* Students experiencing Scripture
* Students understanding their spiritual gifs
* Godly adult examples in every small group
* Students with a hunger for the Word
* Students with a biblical worldview
* Students who are servants
* Students who are wave-makers in the culture
* Accountability
* Creating a missional viewpoint for global impact

If you are the kind of person who is a stickler for detail then you probably counted the two lists and noted that one "top ten list" had eight recommendations and the other had eleven. This does not mean one group was more proficient than the other; it is just a great illustration of how those of us in youth ministry have varied perspectives.

But what is even more obvious is that student leaders know and desire the right things for their youth ministries. The problem in the past was that many of the concepts they espoused in this discussion were not popular in the student ministry paradigm. Youth ministry has accepted too many of the post-modern tenets and consequently we have rendered ourselves less effective.

Youth ministry has accepted too many of the post-modern tenets and consequently we have rendered ourselves less effective.

Let me say that I am excited about what I see and hear as I talk to youth pastors, youth leaders, and parents across this nation and from other countries. Some of the most vocal advocates for change are the "twenty-something's" and "thirty-something's." These two groups are recent products of our youth ministries that did not fall through the cracks. They want to be at the point of the spear of change. They are not afraid to question the status quo and to say it is time to approach student ministry with this new paradigm.

Another group of people I have found ready for change are parents. They are voicing their desire to work together with youth ministries and others to have the greatest influence on their teens. They are no longer content to stand on the sidelines and they are volunteering at incredible rates. They see the problems firsthand every day and realize it is going to take the entire body of Christ to reach this generation with the truth. Many of them are willing and able to impact their own teens plus expand their influence to other students within the youth ministry if they are given some biblical instruction.

The good news is that pastors, parents, youth leaders, and even students realize we have to adjust and want change. This is more than a cultural shift; it is an embracing of solid biblical principles that should be foundational for our lives and ministries. By observing the brainstorm lists, and through reading numerous articles and books on youth ministry, I would like to condense some re-occurring principles that are taking shape in ministries where biblical life-change is the goal.

INTENTIONAL LIFE-CHANGE MINISTRY MODEL

* Teach solid biblical content, including doctrine, not just the current trends. For too long, doctrine has been viewed as too difficult for students but the reality is that they can "get it."

* Develop students to take responsibility for their own spiritual walk with Christ and realize the value of accountability. Leadership by example in this area is strategic.

* Train adults to be godly leaders who do "life-on-life" discipleship. This will include defining an individual strategy for each student for his or her spiritual journey. While this may appear to be overwhelming and time-consuming, leaders are grasping the concept of preventative ministry rather than reactionary ministry.

* Create partnerships between parents and youth ministry to prepare students for real life. The extreme viewpoints of student ministry being performed by parents only or church youth leaders only are being abandoned. Churches are embracing a "both/and" mindset and are rejecting the "either/or" philosophy.

* Develop students with a biblical worldview who are culture-shapers and have a vision for global impact. A biblical worldview is more than just how you live every day; it is foundational to the Christian life. Discovering the moorings of one's faith creates a strong platform for shaping culture.

* Answer real-life questions with the truth of Scripture and demonstrate how this can be fleshed out in daily living. Students who know answers to the questions of "What?" "Why?" and "How?" are stronger in their faith.

I am not purporting that these are all-inclusive, but they definitely represent a transformation in direction.

The idea is that we need to have intentional ministry that is focused on life change, not life management.

The idea is that we need to have intentional ministry that is focused on life change, not life management. These six tenets can serve as the foundation for the preparation of a biblical ministry strategy that could eradicate the revolving door of youth ministry.

In 2 Timothy 2:2, Paul not only gives us a great plan for world evangelization but his words also serve as a model for cultivating students of influence. Paul says, "The things which you have heard from me in the presence of many witnesses, entrust these to faithful men who will be able to teach others also." (NASB95)

From Paul's words I have extracted three concepts to provide a strategic template for cultivating students:

ENLIST – "entrust these to faithful men"

EQUIP – "who will be able"

ENGAGE – "to teach others"

Cultivating students of influence should be more than a maxim or mantra; it needs to be our passion. The biblical plan is about growth through multiplication, not just addition. It is not enough to reach students and just "hang on" to them until they graduate. We must be transforming them into culture-shapers and world-changers every step of the way. Our goal is to reproduce reproducers of the faith.

Our goal is to reproduce reproducers of the faith.

ENLIST

For many years, Uncle Sam has been recruiting and enlisting for the armed services. The campaigns have used everything from posters with Uncle Sam's over-exaggerated finger pointing outward saying, "I want you!" to the current commercials showing how elite this group of recruits will be. My point is that there is a plan for enlistment. As the culture has changed, the appeal has changed, but the cause has remained the same.

I think particularly for this generation it is imperative that we answer some of their questions right up front. The advertisements do just that in that they tell the audience what they will be doing, why they will do it, and what it will look like. They promote the concept of individualizing their training while being a part of something big. Not a bad pattern for us to mirror as we enlist students to the greatest cause in life.

What exactly are they enlisting to do and to be?

The commercials are sometimes flashy and make the work look glamorous. I am not suggesting we follow this lead. Too many young people have joined the ranks under false pretenses of what it means to be a disciple so I recommend we tell the truth about the cost of discipleship. They need to know that we are in a spiritual battle. Serving the Lord is the greatest thing in the entire world but not every day is fun.

At the same time, we do not need to back up our "gospel dump truck "and unload everything at the same time. I am glad God has allowed me to discover His will over a multi-year period. If I had known as a teen everything I know now about God's plan for my life, I would have been scared to death. We need to introduce them to this adventure but not necessarily explain about all the charging rhinos.

One of the best ways to communicate our point is to show them the truth of commitment in our own lives. It is much easier for them to get the big picture if they can see an example. I have often wondered if more students would not step up and out for Christ if they saw more of us in leadership doing the same.

Is it worth it?

After speaking to a large group of students at a camp, several of them surrounded me with some very penetrating questions about committing their lives to Christ. Some of the questions were the normal ones you hear all the time, but then one young man looked me right in the eyes and asked, "Is it worth it?" The undivided attention of every student in the group turned toward me as they waited for my answer.

I already knew that my answer was going to be met with another question but I gave it anyway, "Emphatically yes! Yes, it is worth it!" His follow up question was, "Why?" and before I could answer he said, "I want to know how this works in your personal life." I am not going to give my entire speech here but I do want you to know that I was glad that this was not just another "Christian cliché" with me, but the passion of my heart.

If we are going to enlist students then they need to see our passion and that God has given a purpose to our life. This generation is attracted to a cause. They may not define the cause the exact way we do, but the good news is that God has an individual plan for each person and once we discover His purpose, then personalizing the plan is very viable.

This generation is attracted to a cause.

EQUIP

Equip them with truth

The process of equipping students involves more than having a program led by a personality. Both program and personality are important but they have to be guided by the principles of Scripture. Our plan for cultivating students of influence is based on teaching them the truth of God's Word. I am not suggesting a checklist of doctrinal and topical content but I am saying that having a biblical scope and sequence for our ministry communicates that we have given careful analysis to the only thing that is not a variable in their lives.

Students can grasp doctrine if we as leaders carefully prepare our studies and communicate clearly. A casual perusal of the subjects they study in high school today will reveal that they are accustomed to deep matters and content. I do not think doctrine has to be difficult or complicated. I believe students want to understand the foundations of their faith.

I believe students want to understand the foundations of their faith.

Walt Mueller, the founder of Center for Parent/Youth Understanding, wrote in *Youth Worker Journal*, "Teach them how the authoritative Word speaks to every area of life, going to great lengths to speak God's truth on the matters to which they are deferring to the authority of their feelings." [2] Walt has struck at the heart of the matter: if they do not found their lives on the unchanging Word, their feelings will guide them. Students find themselves in a pluralistic, feelings-oriented society today.

Equip them for life

I was blessed when I was given the responsibility of leading a youth group in my local church with a great leadership team. We became a close-knit family and enjoyed spending time together in and out of ministry. We met on a regular basis to plan the ministry, including the lessons, the décor, promotions, activities, and outreach events.

In one of the very first meetings, we talked through every student in the group. We tried to identify where they were spiritually and what we thought their capacity for growth would be. Every meeting we would evaluate our "growth plan" and share about challenges or blessings. I admit that I did not fully understand the value of this at the time, but I have come to realize that this is truly the process of discipleship.

Discipleship is not "one size fits all," so in order to meet every student where they are and move them forward in their faith, we must formulate a "growth plan" or strategy for each student. You may be thinking, "You do not know how many students I have in my ministry." You are right. I do not know the number but I know that every one of them matters to God and that they all need to grow spiritually. The principles do not vacillate; however the process will be unique and personalized.

Obviously this is only going to take place if you reproduce yourself in other leaders. This is covered in more detail in another chapter but let me say that you cannot do this alone. Experience has shown me the average leader can only disciple five or six students effectively. Even then, ministry will be taking place at varying degrees. Those of us in leadership must work together to cultivate students of influence.

We must remember we are building a life, a complete life. This is not an assembly line where we simply attach our widget to the machine and then send it down the line to someone else. In his book *Christian Education*, Lawrence Richards says, "The "training" of a disciple focuses on making the disciple a complete person, a mature believer. As Jesus lived with and taught the Twelve, He was concerned about transformation: His goal was the nurture of life."[3]

We are equipping them to live a life that will be pleasing to God. We need to give them tools to know how to make decisions based on the Word of God and how to be discerning when confronted with error. Often we simply give them a list to memorize rather than a grid to use in judging the difficult matters of life. Not every area of life is addressed with a "thus says the Lord," but every area is covered by biblical principles that can be mined from the depth of God's Word.

ENGAGE

If you have had any Christian education training, you probably read *The Seven Laws of the Teacher* by John Milton Gregory. One of the laws he addresses is the "Law of Expectations," and while I might not totally agree with everything he says, I like this concept.

We have sold our students short. We look at them as though they are in a holding pattern of life and must wait for a later time to be productive and have influence. The world has imposed this philosophy on us and we have jumped on board a train to nowhere. The time for teens to have influence is now. Do not get the idea by the title of this book that cultivating students of influence is only about the future; it is about the present.

Engage students with adult leadership

Every student in your ministry should have a small group leader who is personally responsible for overseeing the mentoring or discipleship process in their life. I am not implying that they replace the parents; I am saying within the youth ministry everyone should be accounted for by an adult. The best case scenario is when the leader partners with the parents to minister to the teen. Some parents may be AWOL (absent without leave) but that should not be true of adult leadership in your youth ministry.

Engage students with parents

Many parents are deeply burdened for their children and want to be a part of their lives. One of the negatives of our society is that the present culture has made such a distinction between teens and adults, particularly parents, that this seems impossible. Just watch some of the commercials or sitcoms and you will see that the message is clear: "Parents are out of touch and teens do not want them involved in their lives." I do not accept this faulty paradigm and know we can help re-engage teens with their parents.

We need to create forums where the parents and teens are together, not always separated. We need to keep the parents informed and involved with the student ministry through the meetings, activities, and outreach. When we accept a position of leadership in a youth ministry, we need to be keenly aware that ministry to parents is included in that commitment.

When I am training youth leaders in local churches, I always encourage them to visit the homes of every student in their small group. There are several very valid reasons for this, such as gaining insight into the teen and connecting with his or her world. But one of the greatest benefits is to explain to the parents that you are an extension of their ministry or influence in the life of their own teen. If they have never really gotten involved in their teen's life, this is a great time to explain the team concept of parent and youth leader.

This is also a great opportunity for you to minister to the parents. Some may be unsaved, others uncommitted to walking with Christ, and some may be just trying to get by. Regardless of their condition, this could be a turning point for the entire family. While you are visiting, take the opportunity to explain what you will be doing in the youth ministry and what some of your goals are for their son or daughter. You will find that in most cases, the support level for your youth ministry will escalate following one of these meetings.

Engage students with students

You may be thinking, "Hey, they are already engaged with other students." You are right but sometimes it is with the wrong students or in wrong scenarios. We want to help construct a plan to expose them to a variety of opportunities to expand their vision and allow "iron to sharpen iron."

This process will take on many formats and can be implemented in multiple venues. Because most of these are addressed by other authors in other chapters, I will just list some of the potential ideas you might want to consider in your ministry:

* Small group discipleship
* Work groups
* Short-term missions trips
* Attending youth conferences

* Evangelistic outreach
* Community service projects
* Discipleship of a younger believer
* Student brainstorming and planning sessions

Engage students with the culture

It would be difficult to be a student in the present society and not be immersed in the culture. They are bombarded every day by the messages of a pluralistic worldview that promotes license without limits, tolerance without boundaries, rationalization without reality, and freedom without responsibility.

Our goal is to equip them in such a way that they can engage the culture, not as pawns on a chessboard, but as master chessmen. They need to understand the culture, but also be armed with the tools of biblical thinking that allow them to engage to influence, not be influenced. For too long, we have tried to protect them from the culture and it is time to engage them as culture-shapers.

For too long, we have tried to protect them from the culture and it is time to engage them as culture-shapers.

Engage students with discipleship

I have already mentioned it but discipleship of every student must be our ultimate goal. Intentional life-change ministry will reject the hypothesis that it is enough to have faithful attendees or groupies. When the model for the ministry is discipleship, then every activity, program, idea, and goal will be judged by this grid and all of the ministry will be elevated to a new level.

I want to suggest that we establish a discipleship plan for every student. I also believe that as they grow in this process, they need to practice 2 Timothy 2:2 and begin to disciple others as well. A discipleship strategy for every teen should include the long-term goal of them reproducing reproducers as well. As they engage in discipleship, often clarity for their own life's purpose will unfold.

So what's next?

As you continue through this book, you are going to be exposed to some great content but you are also going to discover some practical steps to implement in your personal life and ministry. The next step will be to determine to embrace the new paradigm regardless of what anyone else does. It will be to make a commitment to a life-on-life ministry that will require a great deal of investment, but will result in life-change.

REVIEW QUESTIONS

1. What does it mean to reproduce reproducers according to 2 Timothy 2:2?

2. What are some of the ways I can feed myself spiritually?

3. Do you have someone who is holding you accountable for your spiritual growth?

4. If not, who are some people (both at the peer level and from those who are more spiritually mature) that you would consider asking for help? List them.

5. Have you personally made a commitment to grow spiritually and live for Christ?

6. List three areas that you are helping equip someone else to be a better Christian or witness?

7. What two things are you doing to engage in ministry?

CHAPTER 2

Beneath the Surface:
Being All that God Created You to Be

I want you to think about your greatest asset. Are you thinking about the home in which you have invested? Perhaps it's your education, or maybe some stocks and bonds, or it's your 401K or some other retirement program of which you are a participant. Perhaps when you think of your greatest asset you reflect on a relationship with family and friends.

Many people believe that some material asset provides the greatest value in their portfolio. Think of the following example: if you picked the right stock you would be worth a fortune. In 1998 if you invested $10,000 in Apple stock, it would have been worth over $550,000 by 2007![1] And investment in people and relationships is vital to our survival as well.

God tells us in Scripture what we should value as our greatest asset. Proverbs 22:1 says, "A good name is to be chosen rather than great riches, Loving favor rather than silver and gold." Your character, which is described as a good name in this proverb, is really your greatest asset. You may have great wealth and multiple relationships but without character, you are deficient.

As I have participated in student ministry over the last twenty-five years, I have noticed that those who make the greatest impact have the greatest character. Their character and integrity provide the marked difference in their life and ministry. Character is the foundation for building good relationships and even making honest business deals.

Those who make the greatest impact have the greatest character.

Think about those who have influenced you. Most likely they are those whom you have respected and whose opinions you have valued through the years.

John Maxwell says it this way: "What makes people want to follow a leader? Why do people reluctantly comply with one leader while passionately following another to the ends of the earth? What separates leadership theorists from successful leaders who lead effectively in the real world? The answer lies in the character qualities of the individual person."[2]

My prayer is that as you read this chapter, it will challenge you to realize that your number one priority in student ministry is to make sure that you are a genuine model of godly character for those you lead. If we can model this for students, then they will be able to follow our example. The Scripture says that we are a letter read of all men (2 Corinthians 3:2). We may ask, "Why is character so important?" I think you'll find that character is the quality that separates effective leaders from ineffective ones. It is the thing that attracts others and causes them to want to follow us.

Character is the quality that separates effective leaders from ineffective ones.

CHARACTER IS ATTRACTIVE.

I say it that way because young people want to live for something bigger than themselves. Think about the things teenagers are normally living for such as relationships, clothes, iPods, video games, going to concerts or music in general. I think many of them are asking, "Where is the big cause and who are those that are worthy of being followed?"

I believe that our students are attracted to those with great character. Leroy Eims in his book, *Be the Leader You Were Meant to Be*, talks about the "it takes one to make one" principle.[3] In 1 Samuel 17, the people of God were being taunted by Goliath, the giant. David came along and realized there were no giant-killers in Israel. No one was willing to stand and fight against Goliath. Even Saul, the king, was not willing to stand against the giant's attack. All of a sudden, David decided he did not want the name of the Lord ridiculed. So what did he do? He went out and took five smooth stones with his sling and he took care of Goliath on the spot.

If you continue reading in Scripture you will find giant-killers all over the place in Israel (1 Chronicles 20:4-8). Would there have been these numerous giant-killers in Israel had not David been willing to attack the giant? Character is what separates great leaders from followers. Many will be inspired to great positions of leadership because they see those qualities modeled in their leaders. David modeled this for Israel. You and I must model this for our students and leaders.

The principle is that you reproduce in like kind. If you are going to see the lives of students increase in character, then you have to model it yourself. John Maxwell in his book, *Developing the Leader Within You*, quotes Dwight Eisenhower: "In order to be a leader a man must have followers. And to have followers, a man must have their confidence. Hence, the supreme quality for a leader is unquestionably integrity. Without it, no real success is possible, no matter whether it is on a section gang, a football field, in an army, or in an office. If a man's associates find him guilty of being phony, if they find he lacks forthright integrity, he will fail. His teachings and actions must square with each other. The first great need, therefore, is integrity and high purpose."[4]

I had the privilege of growing up at First Baptist Church in Jacksonville, Florida, under the leadership of Dr. Homer G. Lindsay, Jr. Dr. Lindsay drilled into us all the importance of godly character.

I saw it in him. The inspiring leadership of Dr. Lindsay was so attractive to me. I wanted to follow in his footsteps because of the powerful life and influence he had in my life and the lives of so many others.

Dr. Lindsay believed that the passion and character of leaders determined the success of those who followed. He would say that dead pastors produced dead churches. He would say that a leader must be on fire for Jesus. Over nearly fifty years of ministry, Dr. Lindsay believed passionately in character-driven ministry and consistently demonstrated it by his life.

Your students are searching for godly leadership. They want leaders who are passionate about growing more like Jesus Christ and are modeling the life of a committed Christian in front of them. These are the type of student pastors and leaders that build world-changing students.

CHARACTER IS ATTAINABLE

The wonderful thing about emphasizing and modeling Christian character to our students is that God's Word teaches us that we can grow in our character. In 2 Timothy 2:1, Paul tells young Timothy that he can grow in grace. God can take ordinary people and grow them into leaders of character that make an impact. Think of Moses who felt that he could not speak and yet God used him. Think of Gideon whom God used. Think of the Apostle Paul who persecuted the church and later became its greatest advocate.

God can take ordinary people and build character into their life. I recently heard the story that Chuck Colson told of an associate at Prison Fellowship named Al Lawrence. Al had been a prisoner and had come to know Jesus Christ as his personal Savior. He was helping with a gift distribution at a Washington, D.C. church during the holidays and the former President George H. W. Bush had come to help share in the occasion.

God can take ordinary people and build character into their life.

When Colson introduced Al Lawrence to the President, he realized the power of the Gospel. He said, "Here's the most powerful man on the earth, in conversation with an ordinary person whose life had been changed by Jesus Christ. A former prisoner turned into a man of character." Jesus Christ can totally change our lives and give us the kind of character that our students will want to follow. But how do we gain that character? How do we become the model student-leaders who can make an impact?

HOW TO CHANGE YOUR CHARACTER

So when we decide that we would like to become leaders of character, how do we get that done? How do we change our character? These are some simple suggestions that I hope will be of benefit to you.

The spiritual disciplines of the Christian life are the key ingredients to growing in character. The Scripture says, "But grow in the grace and knowledge of our Lord and Savior Jesus Christ" (2 Peter 3:18). A leader must be disciplined in his walk with the Lord. I suggest these five areas in helping you grow into a leader of character:

The spiritual disciplines of the Christian life are the key ingredients to growing in character.

1. Bible study with application - We simply must get into the Word of God. The Bible says that faith cometh by hearing, and hearing by the word of God (Romans 10:17). The main ingredient that will change us and our young people is God's Holy Word.

2. Prayer - Jesus said, "My house shall be called a house of prayer" (Matthew 21:13). Jesus himself rose early in the morning and spent time in prayer with the Father. There's no way for us to change our character unless we spend quality time and quantity time in prayer.

3. Scripture Memory - The Scripture says, "Your word have I hidden in my heart, That I might not sin against You" (Psalm 119:11). As we memorize God's Word we find true success. Joshua discovered this as did David the Psalmist. Hiding God's Word in our hearts brings victory like nothing else.

   This can change us as we target areas of weakness. These weaknesses can be transformed as we memorize Scriptures applicable to these particular needs. Scripture memory is not just for little children, it's for student workers, pastors, and all leaders who want to grow in character.

4. Fellowship in a Good, Bible-Believing Church - This environment of encouragement is contagious in the Christian life. As we fellowship with those who love Jesus, we will grow in our character and love for the Lord as well. By the way, this is not just attending services but it is identifying other men or women of character and establishing relationships with them.

5. Accountability - The Bible says, "Iron sharpens iron" (Proverbs 27:17). Relationships of accountability will impact weaknesses in our life. We all need to find someone who will hold us accountable. This is someone we respect and who is close enough to ask us the hard questions; someone who knows our character flaws and is committed to helping us mature in our faith.

I highly recommend Rod Handley's book entitled *Character Counts: Who's Counting Yours?* This entire book is written on the subject of accountability and it's a powerful tool, particularly in the life of men. I encourage student leaders to read it and to consider the power of accountability in building your character. If we want to get serious about being changed from the inside out and being authentic in our leadership, we must take seriously this issue of accountability.

Dr. Waylon Moore, in his book *The Power of a Mentor,*[5] speaks about the importance of having three relationships that impact your discipling and mentoring. He says everyone needs a pacesetter, someone ahead of him, to guide and direct and challenge him. Everyone needs a peer, someone beside him, as a comrade to encourage him. And everyone needs a pupil, who is someone following him. Your relationship and leadership to your pupil will be greatly enhanced if you have a pacesetter that is holding you accountable and encouraging you.

HOW TO HANDLE QUESTIONABLE ACTIVITIES

In my personal experience as a student minister, I have found that not every question students ask have clear-cut answers from Scripture. Some call these the gray areas and others refer to them as preferences. Regardless of what you call them, the way we personally handle them and teach our students to handle them will greatly affect our leadership potential and the lives of our students.

Sometimes it's lonely to be a leader of students. Our convictions and commitments have to remain strong if we are to truly impact our students in a powerful way. I have found it best to communicate that some issues are just not addressed with a "thus saith the Lord." In those times, we need to provide a template for making godly decisions that promote character. Consider the following questions when facing difficult decisions about your lifestyle and character. These may not be new to you but I have found them helpful. Ask yourself:

1. Is it helpful? See 1 Corinthians 6:12. Is it helpful to me physically? Is it helpful to me spiritually?

2. Does it have the power to control me? See Romans 6:13 and 16. Does it enslave me? Anything that can control my life should be left alone.

3. Will it cause others to stumble? First Corinthians 8:12-13 points out that I may be the only example of a Christian that others see so I must think of others instead of myself.

4. Is it glorifying to God? First Corinthians 10:31 says in whatever we do, do it all for the glory of God. Is what I'm considering as a habit or action going to glorify the Lord Jesus Christ? God's Word provides the challenge that can change my character. The Book of James talks about God's Word being the mirror I look into that causes me to make adjustments in my spiritual life.

CONCLUSION

I had the privilege of knowing a student worker, a lay leader in our church, who worked with students for over fifty years. His name was Howard Marshall. Howard was a man who was saved on the bow of a ship during WWII. He gave his heart and life to Jesus Christ. He moved back to Jacksonville, Florida, and began working with high school students. He actually was recruited by one of the leaders in our church to "just fill in," and the rest is history. Through the years, Howard Marshall taught many young men.

For a large part of his service, he taught young men who were seniors in high school. I remember not long after I gave my life to Jesus Christ, before my junior year of high school, Howard became my Sunday school teacher. I cannot remember very much of the details of the lessons that he taught, but I can remember that whenever he talked about Jesus, his lip would quiver and his eyes would fill with tears because he loved Him so much. As a young man looking for answers and trying to decide whether to submit my life to the Lordship of Christ, I remember thinking, "I want to have a relationship with Jesus like him." His character and his love for Jesus were attractive to me as a young man.

You can imagine what I felt like when I went back to First Baptist Church of Jacksonville as the student pastor. There he was, my Sunday school teacher, Howard Marshall, still teaching. He could hardly go anywhere in Jacksonville and not see someone who would say, "Hey Mr. Marshall, you taught me when I was a senior in high school at First Baptist." What a legacy.

Howard Marshall was not necessarily the most skilled teacher I've ever met. He's not necessarily the most eloquent communicator that I've ever met. One thing is for certain, he has a legacy of young people who have fallen in love with Jesus, largely due to the fact that he was a man of character. When all is said and done, I will take character over financial prowess, because truly when I think of impacting student lives, I'm reminded once again that a good name is rather to be chosen than great riches, and loving favor rather than silver and gold.

Towards the latter years of Howard Marshall's tenure as high school Sunday school teacher I asked him to speak to our youth workers. He shared with them that his desire was simply to build a bridge to young people that would influence their life. He quoted this wonderful poem that has meant so much.

THE BRIDGE BUILDER

By Will Allen Dromgoole

An old man, going a lone highway,
Came, at the evening, cold and gray,
To a chasm, vast, and deep, and wide,
Through which was flowing a sullen tide.

The old man crossed in the twilight dim;
The sullen stream had no fears for him;
But he turned, when safe on the other side,
And built a bridge to span the tide.

"Old man," said a fellow pilgrim, near,
"You are wasting strength with building here;
Your journey will end with the ending day;
You never again will pass this way;
You have crossed the chasm, deep and wide-
Why build you a bridge at the eventide?"

The builder lifted his old gray head:
"Good friend, in the path I have come," he said,
"There followeth after me today,
A youth, whose feet must pass this way.

This chasm, that has been naught to me,
To that fair-haired youth may a pitfall be.
He, too, must cross in the twilight dim;
Good friend, I am building the bridge for him."[6]

REVIEW QUESTIONS

1. How does Proverbs 22:1 describe character?

2. On a scale of one to five, how much influence do you think you have because of your character right now?

3. Name one person you would view as a model because of their character.

4. List three qualities of their life that attract you to them?

5. What two actions or attitudes will you change to develop your character?

6. Write in fifteen words or less what you would want people to say about you at your funeral.

CHAPTER 3

A Discipleship Strategy for the Real World:
Reproducing Student Disciples

To actually watch a student's life change is an incredible experience. But to know that God used you as an instrument to facilitate life change is overwhelming. It is such an amazing concept that most of us feel inadequate or undeserving to be a part of this change. However, we are all called to do just that. Why do you think we are left here on Planet Earth? Yes, it is to glorify God, but how do we do that?

Paul explains to the Philippians, "For to me, to live is Christ, and to die is gain. But if I live on in the flesh, this will mean fruit from my labor; yet what I shall choose I cannot tell. For I am hard-pressed between the two, having a desire to depart and be with Christ, which is far better. Nevertheless to remain in the flesh is more needful for you" (Philippians 1:21-24).

Did you capture that? Paul struggled with his destiny and concluded that the reason for his existence was to disciple others. While you may completely agree with this model, you may feel a bit inadequate because you do not have the title Apostle in front of your name like Paul. You don't walk around with a following and you can't raise people from the dead! Now that would be life change!

In John 14:12, Jesus makes a remarkable statement: "Most assuredly, I say to you, he who believes in Me, the works that I do he will do also; and greater works than these he will do, because I go to My Father." What are the greater works? Bottom line: evangelism and discipleship, which equals life change. By Jesus dying and rising again, we have the privilege of sharing the Gospel of Jesus Christ and watching something more incredible than feeding the five thousand. We get to witness life change in another individual; to see them turn from darkness to light and then to continue to grow in the knowledge of God. Since the days Jesus walked on this earth, multitudes beyond anything seen during His time on earth have been evangelized and discipled.

If you are saved, I know you have a hunger to bring glory to God and to influence others. The Holy Spirit of God Who dwells within you instills that passion within your heart. But many people squelch that desire for the following three reasons:

1. Fear

In order to witness life change, you need to build relationships. Relationships are synonymous with risk. Rejection is always a potential. All the "what ifs" come to mind: What if they don't listen to me? What if they ask a question I can't answer?

In order to witness life change, you need to build relationships.

What if I give a wrong answer? And the list goes on and on. Maybe some of you tried discipleship before and have been burned—join the club! Remember, Jesus had twelve disciples and one of them betrayed him after three and a half years! It is okay to be afraid, but don't let it stop you from doing the will of God!

2. Failure

Have you ever thought, "How can I disciple anyone to holiness when I know how much of a failure of a Christian I am?" You may be right. You fail in your faith, in your patience, in your Quiet Time, in listening, and to be honest, you may be one big failure covered in a few Christian clichés! Fortunately, I don't see anywhere in Scripture where it says that you cannot disciple or be used by God until you have reached perfection! God is not looking for perfection, but humility! I am amazed how many Old Testament kings reigned in wickedness, but then humbled themselves before God and then He blessed them! James 4:10 says, "Humble yourselves in the presence of the Lord, and He will exalt you" (NASB95). But just a few verses before this he states, "God is opposed to the proud, but gives grace to the humble" (NASB95). I have come to realize by personal experience that when I let failure stop me from getting involved, it is really a form a pride. God actively opposes the proud. I really don't need God opposing me, do you? I need His grace, but that only goes to the humble, to the one who says, "God, this isn't about me, but You through me." So when you fail, confess your sin and get back into the game. Don't let failure equal quitting.

Don't let failure equal quitting.

3. I don't know how

You don't know how many youth ministries I have sought to help only to learn they don't have leaders. Sound familiar? What I have found to be true is that many who would be leaders won't volunteer until they know what they are getting themselves into. People get excited about an idea but are not interested in giving a blank check of time and effort. They want to see a plan in action.

What about today — how do we take this principle from Paul and apply it? How do we get life change in students? In my twenty-seven years of ministry I have seen many different strategies implemented to answer this question. Let's discuss the three more popular strategies that I have observed. They may all contain some good concepts but in my opinion, they all fall short of a biblical strategy.

STRATEGY № 1 — STRONG CENTRALIZED PROGRAM

In this strategy, we pour all our efforts into one major program. It can be on a Wednesday night, Friday night, or Sunday morning. Timing is irrelevant. The point is that it is *big*. The idea is not to get into the students' lives but to get students. So we find a great student band or top-of-the-line song leader, install great lighting and theatrics, and then broadcast the message through a personality. You get extra bonus points for having a theme run throughout the night. I am not saying that numbers, lighting, bands, or personalities are wrong, just that they are not enough.

STRATEGY №2 —
DECENTRALIZED SMALL GROUPS

In this strategy, we pour all our efforts into establishing small groups. Sometimes they meet around the church; others around town. You can run these for Sunday school or any other time of the week. The point is to divide and to conquer. To meet with just the girls, or just the junior high, or just the... well, you get the idea. Small groups need to be a vital part of our strategy but they must be done intentionally.

STRATEGY №3 —
CORE GROUP VS. EVANGELISM

In this strategy, you have two meetings. One designed for the students who are serious about growing or those you refer to as *core*. You meet with these students to pour your wisdom into them and hopefully help them mature. The group consists of about ten to fifteen percent of your average attendance. Then, on a separate night you gear up for primarily evangelism, but you also invite all the carnal students. Once again, evangelism and core groups have to be considered but they must be part of a larger scheme. Also, let me say that separating these groups really sends a message of superiority and tends to fragment your youth ministry.

Perhaps you have identified your present approach and are feeling a bit defensive. Remember all of these have some great points and I am not going to advocate that you necessarily get rid of them. What I do want to do is examine a model for true discipleship.

Did you ever notice how many times Jesus used the "centralized approach" in ministry? You can see it in the Sermon on the Mount, feeding of the four thousand and the five thousand, and even in the cleansing of the temple. But this was not His only means of provoking life change.

How about Jesus' use of "small groups"? We see Jesus meeting with the woman at the well, spending one-on-one time with Peter, John, Lazarus, Mary, and Martha, or talking personally with the blind man or with the centurion whose son was sick. During these times He would share great truths such as salvation, commitment, or His resurrection and we witness life change or rejection of His truth.

We all would expect Jesus, Who is God, to do this but what about common people like me? So I suggest you consider Timothy and Epaphroditus, Titus, Philemon, Mary, Eunice, or even the woman at the well. The greatest impact that you will have on others' lives is when you can get one-on-one and personally walk with them through personal spiritual growth.

Do we need large fantastic meetings that capture the imagination of students and inspire them with an incredible message? Yes! Do we need small groups of students to receive more personalized teaching? Yes! Do we need special evangelistic meetings? Absolutely! But, if I could do only one thing—it would be to personally disciple others, one-on-one.

Still not convinced? Stop and take inventory of your life. Look at the spiritual mile markers. While there are some markers as a result of great meetings, most exist because someone took you aside one-on-one and confronted you, encouraged you, exhorted you, chastened you, or all of the above. When I stopped for a minute and thought about the men who took time for me and poured into my life, I realize I am a blessed man.

Stop and take inventory of your life.

DISCIPLESHIP-BASED STRATEGY

So how can we make this practical and applicable to where you live today? In order to catch this realistically, let's create an average-sized youth group of thirty teens. Don't skip to the next chapter if your youth group is bigger or smaller. I have worked with groups of five to six and groups of over one thousand. The principles here will work no matter how big or small the youth group.

Often we are comfortable because we have thirty teens in our youth group and have a youth pastor or youth leader. That is all we need right? Wrong! I believe the primary function of a youth pastor or youth leader is not to the students, but to his team. I call it "trickle down discipleship."

Think about it: how many people can an average person disciple? I mean, life change discipleship? I have discovered by experience that the average for a full-time youth worker is about six students. Many of our youth workers have a full-time job so we may be talking about a few less. So, we have a youth pastor or youth leader with thirty students but he can only effectively disciple six. How do you keep the others coming? Perhaps he uses great music videos, crazy games, and a lot of entertainment, and while all these can be used beneficially, they do not make for a balanced ministry. So let me suggest a plan:

Step One — Recruit one leader for every five students you have in your group.

That means, in your youth group of thirty, you need to find six leaders. I know, you tried and you can't, right? By the way, this is a problem in large and small churches. I was consulting a large church sharing this philosophy. When I told them how many they needed, they said they would never be able to recruit enough. Not many youth ministries have a leader unemployment line or waiting list.

But here is the key to recruitment. Lay out the plan I am sharing with you and communicate it to the other workers in your group, parents, and prospects. Be aggressive in getting leadership. Proper leadership is indispensable to a successful discipleship ministry. New leaders will be available if they know you have a strategy and the tools to equip them for the ministry. Make prayer a priority for recruitment. In twenty-seven years of consulting churches in youth ministries, I have observed that when churches get serious about getting leaders, the Lord provides.

Proper leadership is indispensable to a successful discipleship ministry.

Step Two — Evaluate the students in your group.

I would divide your students by sex. Then put them into three groups. Identify your hot, on-fire students and your cold, carnal students. If your church percentages hold to the average then you will probably find that you will have about six students in each category. This leaves about twenty left over. (I know, technically eighteen, but twenty sounds better!) I like to call these "mugwumps" and I know it is a dumb name but trust me, you'll remember it! Mugwumps are fence-riders, middle-of-the-roaders. These students wouldn't get excited if you went to Disney World, Six Flags, and ended the day with the Rapture.

Now that you have divided the students by group, assign them to a leader. Each leader will take four to six students. This might be one hot, one cold, and three mugwumps students—all the same sex as the leader.

If you are the youth pastor or youth leader, then your discipleship group consists of your leaders. You will disciple them and they will in turn disciple the youth. This also frees up the youth pastor or youth leader to deal with those serious issues of students in other discipleship groups that are beyond the ability for the lay-leaders to handle.

Step Three — Evaluate your discipleship group by individuals.

Let me suggest three things to consider in the evaluation of each student. It is not a matter of just looking at all of them as a group but rather as individuals. Remember, you will probably have students at various stages of spiritual maturity and desire so you need to identify their individual levels.

First: Evaluate each one. Determine where they are spiritually in their walk with Christ. I know this is like "fruit inspecting" but even Jesus said, "By their fruits you shall know them."

Second: Now that you know where they are, determine where you want them to be by the end of the year. Think about their capacity for growth and help them set some spiritual goals.

Third: Develop a plan to get them from where they are to where you want them to be. This will take time and some conversations with the students, your other leaders, and their parents. Let's walk through some examples.

Develop a plan to get them from where they are to where you want them to be.

Student 1 — Lost Larry

You have Lost Larry in your group. He comes once in a while when forced by his mom. So, where is he spiritually? Nowhere, he is lost! Where do you want to see him by the end of the year? Saved! So what is the plan to get him there? You want to share Christ personally with him or how about inviting him to an evangelistic night at your church, or take him to a Christian concert with his favorite genre of music? Figure out a plan that will introduce him to Christ.

Student 2 — Carnal Carl

Carnal Carl usually just sits there slumped in his chair and has a bad attitude. Where is he spiritually? Saved, but not much else! Where do you want him to be by the end of the year? One of the goals would be to have a changed attitude. So, how are you going to get him there? How about taking him out to breakfast one day and discovering what makes him tick? Find out what is causing the bad attitude. You won't be able to do that while others are watching so get him alone.

Student 3 — Mugwump Matt

He is a nice guy who comes faithfully but is more interested in the women than the Word. He is always trying to look cool. Where is he spiritually? Observation says that he is coming to church with his Bible but not much more. Where do you want to see him by the end of the year? I would suggest getting him into the Word doing a quiet time at least four times a week. So what is your plan? How about calling him every school morning and getting him up to spend a few minutes with God? Or picking him up and going to McDonalds before school and doing your quiet time right there together?

Student 4 — Mugwump Mike

Mike's parents just went through a divorce. He just started coming to church. Where is he spiritually? He is saved and loves God but is really hurting. His passion for a godly life has waned since the divorce. Where do you want him to be by the end of the year? You want to help him have a restored passion for God. How are you going to get him there? How about bringing him over to your house and playing video games then letting him talk out his hurt? You give support, Scripture, and prayer. Help him deal with the rejection and bitterness.

Student 5 — Hot Harry

Finally, you have Hot Harry in your group. Where is he spiritually? Harry is a growing, vibrant Christian. He is very responsive to spiritual things. Where do you want him to be by the end of the year? Perhaps teaching a Sunday school class and doing his quiet time every day. How are you going to get him there? Have him talk to your Sunday school superintendent. Get him trained on being an effective teacher. Check on his quiet time every week for accountability.

Did you catch what we just did? We created a customized (very basic) discipleship program for each student in your group. You identified where each one is and where you want them to be and how you are going to get them there. If all six leaders did that then all thirty students in your group would have an individual plan for discipleship. By the way, the youth pastor or youth leader needs to do the same thing for his leaders!

One more thing: a few of you may be wondering what to do if you have many more students in your youth group? The answer remains the same: one leader for every five students. If you have one hundred and fifty students in your group – that would mean thirty leaders. Then I would suggest recruiting what I call five unit leaders. The youth pastor or youth leader disciples the five unit leaders and each unit leader then disciples five leaders. I worked with a youth group of over six hundred using this principle.

Step 4 — Ideas that will stimulate discipleship with your students

Students spell love T-I-M-E.

Students spell love T-I-M-E. It figures right—the very thing you don't have a lot to give. But that is why it is such an incredible gift to give. If time is not on your side, you may have to get very creative. Here are some ideas:

1. E-mail or write on Facebook. Stay in touch every week with a simple note saying you are praying for them.

2. Text them when you know they are hurting or struggling.

3. Buy them their favorite candy. (More of a girl thing, unless it is chocolate!)

4. Give them a call to check on their quiet time.

All of these are easy and fairly non-threatening. They show that you are thinking of them. Let's take it a notch higher on the next list:

1. Take them out to eat for breakfast in order to talk.

2. Bring them over to your house and let them see how you live.

3. Take them to a ball game.

4. Go to their ball games or special events.

Discipleship is simply spending time with someone and taking the opportunities that come to shape and mold them to be more like Christ. But you need to spend time.

Students will not open up right away. Don't expect the student that you choose to all of a sudden open up during your first meeting and pour their entire heart out to you! If that does happen, pinch yourself hard and wake up! Trust takes time. Many times you have no idea that you are making an impact until years later. I remember one discipleship relationship that I had with a young man. Every week I would get him out of bed and drag him to McDonald's and we would do our quiet times while eating a sausage egg with cheese biscuit. He would barely say a word. I'll be honest, by the end of the year, I thought I had failed. Yet, when another leader asked him what the highlight of the year was, he said it was his times with me at McDonald's doing our quiet times! Go figure!

When we think about discipleship, we often think about life change in the student. But what about you? Are you ready to change? God uses a discipleship relationship to develop both the discipler and the disciplee. (I always have to think which is which but you get the idea!) Now let me give you the true secret to discipleship. (Did you

God uses a discipleship relationship to develop both the discipler and the disciplee.

ever notice that when you put the word *secret* into something you are selling, it sells more?) The secret is this: to be successful in discipleship you need three people in your life.

1. You need a Paul. A Paul is someone who will mentor you. They will pour into your life so that you don't become drained and exhausted. This can be your pastor or a godly older lady in your church. If there is no one right now, it can be someone from history. Read biographies and literature of great men and women to challenge you. A Paul is someone who inspires you to keep going even if you don't feel like it.

2. You need an Epaphroditus! Do you remember him in the Book of Philippians? (Many people call this person your Barnabas. I know his name means encourager but I don't see him doing that to Paul! Maybe I just see things differently.) Paul said that Epaphroditus was five things to him in Philippians 2:25. He was a brother, a fellow worker, a fellow soldier, a messenger, and a friend for Paul. This person is one who gets involved in your life. It is a friendship where mutual discipleship occurs. I read once that the average pastor talks to another pastor about once every six weeks. We all need more encouragement and fellowship than that. It is important to find someone who will get involved in your life and keep you accountable to stay faithful.

3. And finally you need a Timothy. When you think discipleship, this is where everyone goes first. But can you see that if you have a Paul and an Epaphroditus in your life how much more effective you will be with your Timothy.

Leroy Eims in his incredible book, *The Lost Art of Disciple Making,* makes this incredible statement: "What then did He mean in His prayer when He said, 'I have finished the work'?"[1] When you read the prayer carefully, you'll notice that He did not mention miracles or multitudes, but forty times He referred to the men whom God had given Him out of the world. These men were His work. His ministry touched thousands, but He trained twelve men. He gave His life on the cross for millions, but during the three and a half years of His ministry He gave His life uniquely to twelve men."

What a powerful example for us all to follow!

REVIEW QUESTIONS

1. What did Paul realized was his destiny here on earth?

2. If discipleship is so important to our Savior, why don't more Christians do it?

3. How many students can a leader really disciple? How many are you currently attempting to disciple?

4. Who are the three people who you need in your life to be an effective discipler?

5. On whom does God work to see life change in a discipleship relationship?

CHAPTER 4

The Freedom of Intentional Living:
Managing More Than Your Time

If you have spent much time around students and their families, the following story may sound familiar:

> "It has been 12 days since Mom, Dad, Erich, Janey, and Melissa Morgan had a meal together.
>
> No, Dad is not out of town, and no one is angry. They did not plan it this way, but they figure that is just the way life is today.
>
> You see, Erich's bus leaves for high school at 7:05 a.m. Janey leaves for middle school at 7:40. Mom takes Melissa to elementary school at 8:45 a.m. and then she is off to work. She works part time so she can be with the children: in reality, the only time she is "with" the children is when she is in the van. She feels more like a taxi driver than a mom.
>
> Janey, one of the top acrobatic and jazz dancers in her troop, has advanced dance class after school on Monday, Tuesday, and Thursday until 6:00 p.m. (with an occasional Saturday morning rehearsal thrown in).

Erich's high school basketball team, off to a two and seven start, is practicing overtime every day after school except on days when there are games.

Melissa wants to be a dancer like Janey, so she practices with the beginner group, as soon as Janey's class is over.

Monday night is church visitation. Wednesday night there are church activities. Sunday night is church, too, of course. Almost every Friday or Saturday night at least one of the children is spending the night with a friend. And, Saturday is lawn day, basketball games, dance performances . . . the list is endless.

Mom is taking a computer course on Tuesday evenings. Some of Dad's clients insist on dinner meetings. There seem to be two or three a week.

Perhaps you recognize this family. Stretched, stressed, and losing touch with each other. The family is easy to find. It lives in your neighborhood, on your block, maybe in your house. You do not want to raise your family like the Morgans."[1]

Reading that story exhausts me. But it resembles far too many families today. This is not the story of a spiritually disinterested or unchurched family. This describes the way many who love Jesus with a passion live their lives. We live in a culture that has made busyness a part of so-called success. That disposition has filtered to our children as well. As parents of two teenagers, my wife and I have fought the "busier is better" mentality for years.

In the church, we have made busyness a mark of godliness, although Scripture would not necessarily concur. We are the only country with a Mount *Rush*more, after all. Our attention deficit hyperactivity disorder (ADHD), multitasking culture has not made student ministry easier. Yet in the middle of the frenzy, a heart cry for simplicity has emerged. From the serious, including books like *Simple Church* and *Simpleology,*[2] to the ridiculous with shows like *The Simple Life,* simplicity has emerged in reaction to the whirl of contemporary, frenzied lifestyles.

Ephesians 5:16 tells us to redeem the time for the days are evil. In fact, the Bible says much about time. Yet when we think of spiritual topics to teach youth, a subject like time management hardly comes to mind. Most believers do not think on a consistent basis about the importance of the stewardship of one's time. Wasting time may not be on a top ten list of sins to avoid for the average American believer, but in reality we have no more precious commodity with which to be good stewards than time. You and I can make more money. We can make more friends. We cannot make more time. When this day passes, we will never see it again.

JUST WHAT IS CHRISTIANITY ANYWAY?

When you boil Christianity down to its essence, it is neither a ritual to follow nor merely a rule book to obey. A movement flowing out of a relationship with the Most High God, Christianity is a movement—a movement we spend our lives advancing. Truth matters, because without a message worth dying for, movements quickly die. But the truth we declare is living truth, unchanging in its essence and yet life-changing in its impact. Our involvement in local churches matters, for Jesus loved the church and gave Himself for her. But too many believers today have reduced Christianity to a form of two parts doctrinal code, one part behavior modification, and two parts activity in a church building. You can be considered a great Christian if you show up at church all the time, give money, and serve in some capacity. All those matter. But none of them constitute Christianity at its heart. Giving a little time to the institutional side of our faith does not constitute a biblical Christianity. All our time is God's, so how we spend our time matters.

Truth matters, because without a message worth dying for, movements quickly die.

We are not translated to Heaven at conversion, in no small part so that we can continue to advance the great movement of God through our lives. Jesus' last words to His followers were, "You shall be My witnesses" (Acts 1:8 NASB95). The Book of Acts records the advancement of God's movement. Acts ends rather abruptly, for while the canon of Scripture is closed, the story of the church's movement begun in Acts will continue until it is raptured.

From God's initiative in creation, to His call of Abraham, to the movement of His people into the Promised Land, all the way through the Old Testament, we read of the movement of God among His people. Turn to the New Testament and see how Jesus in the Gospels continually called people to become a part of the movement: "Follow me" flows often from the lips of our Lord. Try to read the Book of Acts and *not* see how the early believers were consumed with advancing a movement, even though it cost many of them their lives.

Read the history of the church and you will see that when she has been most honoring to God, she has been advancing this movement. Read of the Reformation, the Great Awakenings (we call those *movements* of God), the modern missions *movement,* and see how healthy the church is when focused not on maintaining her institutions but on propelling God's movement.[3] Helping students see their lives through the lens of advancing a movement of God will move their understanding of the faith from one of a dozen commitments to a focused life lived for the glory of God. Living an intentional life daily for the glory of God and the sake of the Gospel cannot happen without a proper respect for and evaluation of how we spend our time. No one I have ever met gets excited about time management. But when young people I meet grasp the concepts of following Jesus and advancing His movement, suddenly they begin to think differently about how they spend their time.

I meet so many youth today, especially those who grew up in church, who have become disillusioned with Christianity. Barna discovered that three out of five students in high school, living at home and active in church, plan to stop attending church when they leave home.[4] That is an alarming statistic! I am convinced part of the reason for this comes from the fact that we have created a Christian subculture that sees following Christ as one more part of life rather than the umbrella under which all of life is to be lived. Rather than seeing the life of a believer as being part of a compelling story, duty serves as a motivator for many. So, managing time becomes just one more inconvenience of life instead of a fundamental way to approach life under the lordship of Christ.

We have created a Christian subculture that sees following Christ as one more part of life rather than the umbrella under which all of life is to be lived.

We live in a culture that pushes us to believe that there are three P's that matter the most: *power, position*, and *possessions*. In the church, ministers sometimes boil down their ministry to the three B's: *building, budgets,* and *bodies.* I would submit that a life lived intentionally for the glory of God and the sake of the Gospel will focus not on those but on the three T's: your *time*, your *treasure*, and your *talents.* If you and I can surrender these three to Jesus and live in such a way that these precious resources are invested in advancing a movement of God, we will find the life we seek. We will sacrifice more. We will think of ourselves less. And we will see ministry that bears fruit. While all three of these matter, I want to focus on the one I would argue matters most (and yet the one we speak least about in our churches): living intentionally by how we manage our time.

PRINCIPLES OF TIME MANAGEMENT[5]

Managing time teaches us to manage our lives. You can discover what matters to a person by looking at two books: their checkbook and their calendar. How a person spends his time and money reveals who that person really is. Helping students nail down an approach to life that helps organize their busyness in a way that helps them to live for Jesus must be considered a vital part of those who work with youth. It is simply not enough to teach them to be passionate for Jesus. It is not enough to teach the fundamentals of the faith or the components of a biblical worldview. We must help them take all that and show them how to actually live out their faith with the time and commitments they have. Our failure to do so contributes to the tendency of youth to shipwreck their faith while barely into the adult world.

Volumes have been written and countless seminars have been taught on time management. The following principles simply look at the big picture, in particular how time management relates to our living intentional lives for Jesus.

1. **You have all the time you need.** You do not, nor will you ever, have all the time you want. Some times in the year you may not have time for anything else but the things that truly matter, but you can do what is important. Like faithful attendance in

worship, or talking to people without Christ about His love for them. If you value video gaming above all else, you will make time to play them.

"The bad news is time flies. The good news is you're the pilot." – Michael Altshuler [6]

What you and I need is not more time, but better management of the time we have. A simple exercise: copy the following chart. Make two more copies. For three weeks, simply record how you spend your time. You will likely discover you waste more time than you think.

	SUN	MON	TUE	WED	THU	FRI	SAT
6:00 A.M.	____	____	____	____	____	____	____
7:00 A.M.	____	____	____	____	____	____	____
8:00 A.M.	____	____	____	____	____	____	____
9:00 A.M.	____	____	____	____	____	____	____
10:00 A.M.	____	____	____	____	____	____	____
11:00 A.M.	____	____	____	____	____	____	____
12:00 P.M.	____	____	____	____	____	____	____
1:00 P.M.	____	____	____	____	____	____	____
2:00 P.M.	____	____	____	____	____	____	____
3:00 P.M.	____	____	____	____	____	____	____
4:00 P.M.	____	____	____	____	____	____	____
5:00 P.M.	____	____	____	____	____	____	____
6:00 P.M.	____	____	____	____	____	____	____
7:00 P.M.	____	____	____	____	____	____	____
8:00 P.M.	____	____	____	____	____	____	____
9:00 P.M.	____	____	____	____	____	____	____
10:00 P.M.	____	____	____	____	____	____	____

2. If you don't control your time, someone will. Young adults have so much of their time scheduled for them, particularly those who are in school thirty-five hours a week, play sports, and are active in church. Adults have programmed the lives of students beyond their ability to cope, and then complain that so many exhibit symptoms of attention deficit disorder (ADD). My wife Michelle and I were a bit older than our peers when we had children, so we observed many parents with children a bit older than ours. We were amazed at how exhausted families were going from activity to activity. It seemed they complained more about their schedules than they ever enjoyed them. We decided while our children were small that we would not do activities year round, such as sports. We decided our family mattered more than sports. I am a *huge* supporter of sports as a means to teach about life, but we tried to set the standard early that mom and dad, not activities, would set the calendar.

Summers can be particularly difficult. By the time you plan for youth camp, mission trips, sports camp, and family vacation, the summer is pretty much gone. Add year-round schools and down time has become even rarer for students. You as a leader of students can help them in their time management. How much of the typical student's life is spent at the church building? Can that time be better spent in other ways?

I have a piece of cord 168 inches long. Sometimes when I speak to youth pastors I hold it up. On the cord I have a three-inch piece of tape. The inches represent hours in a week. We all have 168 hours in a given week. The typical student in your ministry will spend around three hours with you at the church. No matter how amazing your programming, how biblical your teaching, or how awesome your ministry, that is not enough time. Students must learn to utilize their time wisely and part of the limited time you have might be better served equipping students in how to spend the other 165 hours. We need to partner with godly parents to help students use their time wisely.

Once a student sees how much discretionary time he or she has, they may have little left. They may physically be unable to have that hour-long quiet time and give an extra five hours a week helping you at church. I would argue an hour a week with a mentor may do more for a student's walk with God then several hours at a few more church events. Wise use of time starts with an honest evaluation of how we spend our time. Can we admit it if we over-schedule our youth ministry to the detriment of those we long to help become Christ-followers? Both questions beg the recognition that we don't have a lot of time ourselves. How do you develop a Christ-following lifestyle in a student with little time for such development?

> "Don't say you don't have enough time. You have exactly the same number of hours per day that were given to Helen Keller, Louis Pasteur, Michelangelo, Mother Teresa, Leonardo da Vinci, Thomas Jefferson, and Albert Einstein."
> -- H. Jackson Brown[7]

3. **Take care of the big rocks.** The story is likely familiar to you. You take a big jar, and get a collection of a few large rocks just big enough to fit in the mouth of the jar, along with some gravel and a bucket of sand. First, pour in the sand, followed by the gravel, and put the rocks in. They won't all fit. Then remove all the material. The next time, put in the big rocks first, then the gravel, and pour the sand last, which will trickle through the jar, filling up the spaces. You will get much more in the jar like that. The point is simple: If you take care of the big rocks, the little rocks and sand will fit. Determine your priorities based on the Word, and fill in the rest after. Some students will determine they cannot work as many hours at the part time job, or play as many sports, if they will be serious Christ-followers. Young people must learn early to make time decisions based on their values instead of following the crowd.

We think of priorities in terms of a hierarchy. God is first, then family, then ministry, then school, and on and on it goes. I would submit that is a faulty approach to understanding priorities. God is not supposed to be the first in a list. God is supreme in all things. Think less of a ladder with God at the top and more of an umbrella with everything in life under it. God is over all. Or, to use the analogy above, God is not the biggest of rocks; God is the jar. Everything that goes in the jar must be done for the glory of God and the sake of the Gospel. He is not only first in the "spiritual" part of our life. He is first in our sports, in our video gaming, in our online time, in our phone conversations, and so forth.

Youth today have mastered the art of "the disconnect," where they can turn on the spiritual engine at the youth meeting but become almost a totally different person when they log onto their MySpace. We have to help them see that lordship means Jesus reigns over everything from the posters in their rooms to the fast food they consume. Most youth have some concept of this, but they think of it in terms of Jesus being a Cosmic Killjoy: if they allow Jesus to reign in those areas, they will have to listen only to music that mentions Jesus every third word, or play only "Christian" video games, or wear Christian tee shirts all the time. That hardly compares to a biblical understanding of lordship. Jesus being Lord means we see the world—our world, and the world around us—through His lenses. It does not have to turn us into thought police, but it does make us more thoughtful. It may mean we lay some video games down, or eat less junk food; but it does so because of an understanding that Jesus has something far better. The goal of a Christian worldview is not to create a generation of Christian geeks so far removed from the culture, so wrapped up in a pseudo-Christian subculture, that it cannot relate to anything not explicitly spiritual. No, the goal of a Christian worldview is to see the world biblically. This means anything that is true, whether explicitly Christian or not—can

The goal of a Christian worldview is to see the world biblically. This means anything that is true, whether explicitly Christian or not—can bring glory to God.

bring glory to God. Therefore, one can bring much glory to God by giving their best effort at football practice, or by learning to use the computer as a tool to encourage others, and so on. Help students to see that the way they spend their time directly reflects the level to which they seek to honor God with their lives.

4. **Make a "stop doing" list.** Part of the fundamentals of calendaring involves a "to do" list. But we don't think hard enough about developing a "don't do" list: stopping the things that eat at our time wastefully.

5. **Start every day early with Jesus.** Give the Lord the best time, not the leftovers. If you plan to spend time with Jesus when you have *time,* you will never spend time with Jesus. All of our time belongs to Him, but we also need to spend time sitting at the table in His presence. Jesus gave His first and best time to His Father. Mark 1:35 tells us He arose early and spent time with His Father. David also arose early to meet with God. Starting one's day focused on the Lord can only help make the day matter. Some students cannot spend large amounts of time in the morning because they must head to school pretty early. But taking only three to five minutes to start the day thinking about living just that day for Jesus can make that day more honoring to Jesus. Encourage students, for example, to make this threefold prayer a daily habit before they get out of bed. Or better, challenge them to slip to their knees first thing and pray the following to Jesus.

Pray for: 1) An opportunity to touch someone for Jesus through actions or a verbal witness; 2) Wisdom to see the opportunity; and 3) Courage to seize it.

Matthew 6:33 tells us to seek *first* God's Kingdom. Starting the day thinking that way helps us to see how such seemingly mundane, "unspiritual" activities, such as ball practice and homework, can be done to the glory of God.

A little advice for parents of students: 1) Every day, do something in your children's world. Every week I help my grade school daughter with her homework. Do I do it because I love it? No, at the end of the day I would rather do something else than more schoolwork. But I do it because it is important to Hannah. And because helping with homework is what a parent (I did not say a mom!) should do. 2) Discover what your children love to do, and regularly do it with them. That shows them they matter to you. Take your daughter roller skating. Shoot hoops with your son. It is really okay that you are pitiful at basketball! Just spend time with him because he loves it.

That being said, what can we do to manage time?

1. **See time management as a spiritual discipline.** How can a follower of Jesus truly walk with Him without seeing that even walking takes time? How can a life be lived intentionally without a concept of managing the most precious commodity we have in this life? The American church has mastered the ability of compartmentalizing everything. Spiritual things (quiet time, witnessing, church attendance, etc) in one corner, material things (job, money, stuff we own) in another, friends in another, school and sports in another, and so forth. Look at the life of any biblical character and see if you see such separation. David did not separate his being a warrior and a poet and a man of God into categories!

   A part of my daily devotional time involves going over my calendar. How I spend my time demonstrates how I glorify God, so why wouldn't I seek the Lord as I decide how I spend my day? If I do so in the spirit of prayer, it may allow me the opportunity to speak to someone about Jesus I would otherwise have missed. We are to live all our lives—not just the spiritual parts—under the Lordship of Jesus!

2. **Challenge students to be young adults about this, not children.** If they are old enough to be responsible to do their homework, they are old enough to keep a calendar. Work with parents on this one. Many churches offer financial stewardship seminars, and this is helpful. Very few offer counsel on being a good steward of time.

3. **This one is pretty simple: get a calendar.** So many students can keep a calendar now on their phone or their computer. Many can still find value in the good old calendar book. The technology is less important than its use. Write down all dates that matter. Now some students simply are wired to follow a calendar. They will voraciously fill it in, post it on their blog, and update it more than they actually do anything with life. Other students see no purpose in this, and will require a little more encouragement.

4. Put in major dates that do not change: Sunday worship, youth meeting, athletic events, and so forth. Then put in the events that are one-time events. Add any assignments for school. Then begin to fill in short-term, individual dates. Make scanning the calendar several times a day a part of life. Include daily to-do or stop-doing lists.

I live a busy life. I teach full-time in a growing academic community, teaching students in the undergraduate, graduate, and doctoral programs. I have a very active family which includes both a college and a high school student and my wife. I speak at about sixty to seventy events a year in twenty or more states and foreign countries. Over half of those events focus on youth, bringing with each event new friends to keep up with online (which takes time as well, as I keep up with literally thousands of young adults via the internet). God has wired me to be active. My wife could not keep my schedule. God has not called her to do so. But I do this not to earn God's favor or to win the applause of men, but because God has given me an insatiable appetite to advance His movement. And yet, in the middle of such activity, I have never been closer to my wife or children, and never been more fulfilled. Why? The answer is simple. Years ago someone taught me to manage my time wisely and to see wasting time as sin. I take a day off every week. I have missed very few of our children's hundreds of ball games. I learned one must not sacrifice their family on the altar of ministry. But I also learned time is too precious to waste.

I don't often quote Charles Darwin. But his quote on time should be heeded: "A man who dares to waste one hour of life has not discovered the value of life." Because we do not value time as one of the most precious gifts from God after salvation, we freely waste it. There is a time to rest. There is a time to play. But time well spent in this life can impact eternity. And teaching that lesson to students can help them spread their wings and soar for Jesus.

Because we do not value time as one of the most precious gifts from God after salvation, we freely waste it.

REVIEW QUESTIONS

1. How can you redeem (buy up) the time as defined in Ephesians 5:16?

2. What are your top three time-wasters? Create a "stop doing" list.

3. Take your calendar and plan the next two weeks. Once you have completed it, ask a friend to evaluate it.

4. What are the non-discretionary (big rocks) requirements in your life (e.g. work, school, or church)?

5. What are the three things you would like to do v discretionary (free) time?

6. Who holds you accountable for your "life-managemen

CHAPTER 5

Bible Study...Moving from What to How:
Handling the Word of God

"I try to help youth to fall in love with the Bible. It is estimated that three out of four evangelical teens say that once they're grown, they'll be done with church. I have to believe that part of the problem is lack of Bible. So I *never* say, "You are the church of the future." We say, "You are the church *now*...a church built on the Word.""

Former NFL player Derwin Gray, founder of The Gathering, a multicultural church in Charlotte, North Carolina

A friend has a plaque on her wall that says, "The two greatest gifts you can give your children are roots and wings." That's what we are doing when we instill in teens a love for God's Word. The Word of God brings life and liberty. Jesus said, "The truth will set you free" (John 8:32 NIV).

When it comes to cultivating in teens an appreciation for Scripture, more is needed than just stories or superficial lessons. Teens today are caught in the crossfire of a battle for their minds and souls. More than ever, they need the solid spiritual food that only the Bible can give, plus an ability and willingness to study on their own. Ephesians

4:14 tells us to grow in our faith so that we will "no longer be children, tossed to and fro and carried about with every wind of doctrine." Judges 21:25 confirms that even in ancient times, people were "prone to doing what was right in their own eyes." That philosophy of relativism is as spiritually empty now as it was then. Christian teens must ultimately decide if they are going to live by the world's rules (which are really no rules at all), or if they are going to live according to God's truth. What will they pursue: conformity or character? Convictions or convenience?

Christian teens must ultimately decide if they are going to live by the world's rules or if they are going to live according to God's truth.

President Ronald Reagan, a man of conviction, believed that knowledge of the Bible was vitally important for the health of a nation. By official proclamation, he named 1983 the "Year of the Bible." In his proclamation he said:

> I, Ronald Reagan, President of the United States of America, in recognition of the contributions and influence of the Bible on our Republic and our people, do hereby proclaim 1983 the Year of the Bible in the United States. I encourage all citizens, each in his or her own way, to reexamine and rediscover its priceless and timeless message.[1]

Here was a man who understood the significance of knowing Scripture.

Charles Spurgeon told the story of a man who came to his church just to hear great music and singing. As soon as the sermon began, the man put his fingers in his ears and would not listen. But the man removed one hand to brush away an insect that flew at him. Just as he did, the preacher's quote from the Bible rang out, "He that hath ears to hear, let him hear." Spurgeon relates that God used the irony of that event to get the man's attention and he became a solid believer.[2] Spurgeon knew the power of God's Word to those who hear. Paul asked, "How shall they believe in Him of whom they have not heard?" (Romans 10:14). The answer is, "They can't." People cannot believe in Jesus if they do not know there is a Jesus in Whom to believe. The Bible is key to both evangelism and discipleship.

Youth workers throughout the United States repeatedly tell me that the average students with whom they interact are biblically illiterate. Need proof? Ask teens to name even half of the Ten Commandments (or where to locate them in the Bible). Ask them why Jesus had to die. Where is the account of how God created the world? In what book would I find the story of Paul's conversion? An important goal of youth ministry must be to rescue a generation of teens who are drowning in an ocean of relativism, a sea of uncertainty. Many Christian teens are led more by their emotions than by God's Word. Our youth need to know they are loved by their Creator and are precious in His sight. Other religions fighting for their souls do not have a living, loving God Who provided the solution for their sin problem. It may sound narrow, but Christianity is the *only* religion that corresponds to reality. Combining the truths of the Bible with logical, critical thinking will

Combining the truths of the Bible with logical, critical thinking will yield a clear understanding that other religions cannot also be true.

yield a clear understanding that other religions cannot also be true. Our youth need to know that you can care for a person even though you disagree with his religious beliefs. In fact, those who care deeply will help their friends think and pray seriously about the implications of their beliefs.

But what does knowing the Bible do for a person in a "practical" sense? The Christian Scriptures alone give solid, positive answers to life's ultimate questions. The Bible provides comfort and strength for the inevitable and numerous tough times. A good friend of mine recalls how Bible verses and traditional hymns were what carried him through the dark nights following his daughter's untimely death. Knowing the character of God—the depth of His eternal love for us—dispelled the anger. The truths of the Bible helped him move from despair to hope.

The majority of teens are egocentric; life is about them. With consistent, solid, prayerful Bible study, they learn that life is about God and their relationship to Him. What they learn in the Bible and at church must touch all areas of their life. Bible study is not a "church thing." It is what Christians do to equip themselves for life's unrelenting struggles. It is part of the whole armor of God (see Ephesians 6:10-17). Even students themselves tell us that they want their Christian faith to touch all of their lives, and they want someone to teach them. They also want to see authentic Christianity modeled with integrity.

Integrity in Greek, means *cut from the same cloth*. So basically, a Christian with integrity is one who is the same at church, at work, on the ball field, at home, or sitting with the TV remote in his hand. A Christian with integrity sees all of life through a biblical worldview: a view of life based on the truths of the Bible, the truths of Who God is and who man is, created in His image.

You probably know the story of *The Emperor's New Clothes*. Why did everyone go along with the story fed to them by the tailor except one boy who spoke the truth? That story's premise isn't too far-fetched. That's the kind of thing that happens when people don't think for themselves and just latch on to what everyone else says. They want to be "politically correct." Scripture however tells us to destroy "arguments and every high thing that exalts itself against the knowledge of God" and that we are to bring "every thought into captivity to the obedience of Christ" (2 Corinthians 10:5). Give them the roots and wings they need. But it will take a little effort, a little thinking, some planning, and a lot of praying.

WORLDVIEWS, BIBLICAL AND OTHERWISE

I recently read about a college student who, after attending a Christian worldview conference, decided to start a study group in her dorm. She said, "More people began to see how applicable worldviews were to what they were learning in the classroom and talking about it with their friends. For many of us, this was our first opportunity to think about our worldviews and realize that because our God is the creator of the universe, his entire worldview was based on reality." One girl in the group admitted that "some of her ideas and assumptions were not biblically based and were harmful."[3]

As we listen to radio, read newspapers and magazines, watch TV, and surf the web, we are bombarded by conflicting philosophies or worldviews. What is a worldview? Basically, a worldview is the set of lenses through which one views all of life. It colors one's understanding of life's experiences. A person's worldview colors everything he does, whether he knows it or not. Ideas are not just interesting thoughts to be tossed around. Ideas have consequences. One's ideas about how and why the world operates—one's worldview—will impact a person's decisions concerning abortion, evolution, marriage—all areas of life, personal and in community.

A study of worldviews is beyond the scope of this chapter. But always keep in mind that the goal of Bible study is not merely knowledge of facts. The goal is transformed lives: young people who are confident in their faith, and whose biblical worldview gives them courage and compassion for others.

To have a biblical worldview, you must first know the Bible and what it teaches concerning God, man, sin, salvation, and even the Bible itself. You must be convinced that the Bible is God's Word, contains the truth, and is trustworthy. How do our teens measure up?

In our previous book, *Pushing the Limits: Unleashing the Potential of Student Ministry,* I quoted Josh McDowell from his book *Beyond Belief* that "almost 80 percent of teens will no longer participate in organized religion/church by the time they reach adulthood."[4] The number of students who are turning from their faiths demonstrates their ill-preparedness for living out their Christianity in a hostile society. The battle for their minds and hearts begins when they are very young. If they do not choose to live with a biblical worldview, then another worldview will take its place. There is no neutral ground, no vacuum.

COMPREHENSION: CHALLENGED BY DOUBTS

After talking to several high schoolers at local churches, I saw a few common concerns about even studying the Bible: "My teacher said the Bible was written down by people, and since people are fallible, the Bible must be also." "The Bible doesn't seem relevant to me. Why should I read it?" "I already know all of the stories in the Bible." "If I do try to read it, I don't know where to start." "It's too confusing—you say a passage means one thing and my friend says another." "There are so many different versions, which one should you believe?"

These are honest questions that deserve solid answers. Indeed, they require answers that point them in the direction of truth and a life-long commitment to it. Lingering questions about the Bible's accuracy can breed spiritual skepticism. Satan will always try to cast doubt on what God says. At the beginning, in the Garden of Eden, he challenged Eve by asking, "Did God really say that?" These seeds of suspicion, unless removed, can grow to strangle a person's faith. Lack of knowledge of the truths in the Bible and misunderstandings about God can open the door to acceptance of the relativism of our age, to a worldview that contradicts the biblical worldview.

At the beginning of any Bible study you should show your students the trustworthiness and authenticity of the Bible. If it is not reliable, then there is no reason to trust it and make it *the* authority of your life, let alone waste time reading a "bunch of old-fashioned stories." Second, they need a plan for studying the Bible. They need to decide where to begin, either in their personal study or in small groups. What will help them both understand and apply what they are reading to their lives? Third, it is important to tackle some of those difficult "contradictory" passages. It is far better to discuss these in your Bible study than to throw the students unprepared to the skeptical wolves. There is always a dilemma that arises when someone says something like he can hate his parents because it is in the Bible—or any number of "interesting" decisions that are made when verses arbitrarily are pulled out of context. So, to put them on the right track, teach them some basics of *hermeneutics*. This is just a scholarly word for *proper, logical, consistent biblical interpretation.*

IT'S THE REAL THING: AUTHENTICITY OF THE BIBLE

For my book *Stand Strong in College* (Carol Stream, Illinois: Tyndale, 2007), I personally interviewed over one hundred college students. These were mostly freshmen and sophomores, not too far removed from their high school and youth group days, representing over three dozen U.S. states. Of those who experienced spiritually dry periods while in college, almost all cited uncertainty about the Bible's authenticity as the starting point of their struggle. Just because a teen comes from an exemplary Christian home or is faithful in youth group does not guarantee that they are adequately prepared for the probable attacks on Scripture they will hear while in college. Readers young and old must handle the challenges they face regarding the trustworthiness of the Bible. Because the truth of Christianity is inseparably bound up with the historicity of the New Testament, we must not only discuss with teens its *content* but also its compelling *credibility*.

Faith is certainly at the heart of our belief in the Bible, but the book that we trust as God's Word is also a superbly written, historically documented work. It was written by real people, in a real period of history, for a specific purpose and message. Many noted individuals have stepped out to prove the Bible wrong. In the process, critical thinkers like C. S. Lewis (a highly respected literary scholar), Lee Strobel (an award winning journalist who earned a law degree from Yale), and Ann Rice (a best-selling author, known for her meticulous historical research), all moved from doubt to belief as their studies bred within them the firm conviction that the Bible is indeed reliable. They (and countless others) have found both internal and external evidence that the Bible is the Word of God.

External Evidence

By external, we mean *non-biblical sources*. The facts are clear: compared to all ancient books (e.g., Homer's *Illiad*, Plato's *Republic*, Caesar's *Gallic Wars*), the Bible has the oldest copies, the most numerous copies, and the most accurate copies.[5] Sir Frederick Kenyon declares:

> It cannot be too strongly asserted that in substance the text of the Bible is certain: especially is this the case with the New Testament. The number of manuscripts of the NT, of early translations from it, and of quotations from it in the oldest writers in the church, is so large that it is practically certain that the true reading of every doubtful passage is preserved in some one or other of these ancient authorities. This can be said of no other ancient book in the world.[6]

The early church fathers quoted the Bible so often that all but eleven verses of the New Testament can be reconstructed from their quotations.[7] The Bible is not myth; it is not a fabrication. Your students need to know that the Bible is infallible and inerrant. Infallible refers *to the fact that it is not misleading.* Thus, Scripture is a safe, reliable guide in all matters. Inerrant means *free from all falsehood or mistakes*, and so the Bible is trustworthy. God Himself says His Word cannot be broken (John 10:35b).

Secular historians and archeologists give support to many of the claims in the Bible. As Nelson Glueck, a well-known Jewish archeologist, wrote, "It may be stated categorically that no archeological discovery has ever controverted a biblical reference."[8] "William F. Albright (called "the father of modern archeology") said, "There is no doubt that archeology has confirmed the historicity of the Old Testament."[9]

Internal Evidence

Within the Bible itself, there is evidence that the Bible is the Word of God. Internal evidence includes such things as prophecies foretold in the Bible which actually came true. For example, over three hundred Old Testament prophecies of the Messiah's first coming were fulfilled by the birth, life, and death of Jesus Christ.[10] George Heron, a French mathematician, calculated that the odds of one man fulfilling only forty of those prophecies are one in ten to the power of 157.[11] That is a 1 followed by 157 zeros. In other words, a statistical impossibility!

The Gospel of Luke stands out in its remarkable accuracy of historical facts. It contains at least seventy different facts revealing the author's knowledge of local places, names, conditions, customs, and circumstances, all which have been verified by historical and archeological research. In his book *The Book of Acts in the Setting of Hellenistic History,* Colin Hemer, a noted Roman historian, confirms Luke's accuracy.[12] Once again, the stones cry out to confirm what the Bible has taught all along. You can easily do some reading to find other examples to share with your students.

Jesus Himself treated the Scriptures as being literally true (see Luke 24:25; John 17:1-17). His disciples and the early church knew nothing but a literal belief in the Word of God. In fact, to believe otherwise forces you to abandon rational thought. You must engage in mental gymnastics, crimes against language, semantical contortions, historical revision, and intellectual grandstanding, not to mention "pulling rank theologically" arguing against the likes of the prophets, the Apostle Paul, Augustine, and Aquinas.

Implications of the Evidence

In response to such evidence and data, teens may say, "So what?" They should know that is a good, honest question. So, the Bible's content and divine origin can be defended by many compelling lines of evidence. The Bible, then, must be true (as it claims itself to be). Great. Why should this matter to a teen? Consider a few things. First, there are disastrous theological consequences resulting from any other view. If God is not powerful enough to clearly communicate and preserve a message, what basis do you have for believing that God is able to do "larger," more difficult things, like saving a soul or providing a home in Heaven? Personally, I want my view of Scripture to be the opposite of Satan's. In Genesis 3:1 he causes Eve to doubt God's Word. The great deceiver works unceasingly to cause you to doubt, to deny, and to disobey God's Word. Satan's goal is deception and death for you. That's another consideration: the reality of Hell. The Bible says it is real. Jesus speaks more of Hell than He does of Heaven. If the Bible is just a collection of vague generalities, then sin, death, and Hell must not be that serious.

Yes, I believe the Bible is true—literally, historically, actually, genuinely, factually, perennially, existentially, and comprehensively. Every person will find out sooner or later that what the Bible teaches is accurate, either in this life or the next.

HAVE A PLAN, STAN: HOW TO STUDY THE BIBLE

Even students who understand the importance of belief in the Bible and accept that it is true still have questions. One of the most common concerns is where to start reading.[13] What do they need to read for encouragement, inspiration, and to become more equipped to help others? I am told that after they read a selection, often they are left feeling like they only understand the story portions. To some, it seems there is nothing new or interesting, and they cannot relate to the Bible. A key to reaching them, then, seems to be relevancy.

Bible study must be more than just facts. We must apply the principles to real life, to the situations these youth are encountering every day

Bible study must be more than just facts. We must apply the principles to real life, to the situations these youth are encountering every day—dating, sex, ethics at school and work, handling emotions, drinking, choice of music and TV programs, godly living, and use of the internet.

Getting Started

Before beginning any Bible study, pray. It is the Holy Spirit who illuminates our minds, giving us the spiritual understanding we seek. James said, "If any of you lacks wisdom, let him ask of God, who gives to all liberally and without reproach, and it will be given to him" (James 1:5). Ask Him to guide you as you decide on a book to study. The Gospel of Mark is a good book because of its conciseness. It presents Jesus as the Suffering Servant. The Gospel of John is strong theologically and presents Jesus as the Son of God. Perhaps your group is interested more in a topical study. Using a concordance and a topical Bible, you can identify passages that relate to a specific area or do a word study.

A careful reading first looks for what the passage meant to the people to whom it was written. From this you glean principles, and these principles can be applied to your own life. As Norman Geisler says, "To interpret we must in every case reproduce the sense the Scriptural writer intended for his own words."[14] And this must be done before we go on to name the relationships between that meaning and ourselves, our country, our day, and our conception of things; that is, before we consider the significance of the text for us.

When studying an entire book, read straight through. This gives a valuable sense of what the author is saying. Many of the New

Testament books are epistles, letters written to churches. Treat the epistles as you do any letter, and read it in one sitting. If possible, read it in both a strict translation and a modern, "looser" paraphrase. Then ask yourself if the passage tells you who wrote it, to whom, when, where, why, and of course, what—what is the main theme? From this, you glean principles which may be applied to your own life. Get in the habit of always keeping paper or a notebook and pen by you to take notes. Some people enjoy journaling their thoughts.

Another technique is to make a list of the events (if applicable) or thoughts in a chapter. Look at the list and see if the events fall into groupings or divisions. Label these divisions. Then think of a theme or subject sentence of that passage. This, in essence, is like writing an outline in reverse. Once you have established the who, what, when, and why as it applies to the original audience, decide on some lessons you think the recipients could have learned from each section. Translate this into principles that could be applied by anyone in any era. To facilitate discussion, phrase the questions in such a way as to encourage discussion rather than a mere yes or no response.

Study Aids (I favor the hard copies)

In addition to the Bible itself, I would encourage each to own hard copies of some basic study aids. It is true that there are plenty of online Bible study resources, many of which are very helpful. But I believe that there is no substitute for spending time before an open Bible, digging into the Word, taking notes, all the while referencing back and forth with an assortment of time-tested study resources. One of the best ways we disciple teens is to teach them to disciple themselves. Make sure that your students know how to find key verses by using their concordance. Tell them that God won't get mad if they write in His Book; it is okay to underline verses and to write notes in the margins of their Bible! Additionally, here are some recommended study tools that will provide great insights and help to all users:

One of the best ways we disciple teens is to teach them to disciple themselves.

A Bible dictionary: There are several good ones available; select one produced by a reputable Christian publisher.

A one-volume concordance: I recommend *Strong's Concordance* or *Young's Analytical Concordance.* You can use these books to look up any word used in the Bible. Note the number given, then look the number up in the back to see the original Greek or Hebrew word.

A Bible handbook: Check out such classics as Halley's Bible Handbook or Willmington's Bible Handbook. Either of these will provide a wealth of information about people, places, history, and just plain interesting facts related to the Bible. Seriously, start reading either of these handbooks and you'll find that they are hard to put down.

A dictionary of New Testament words: Specifically, *Vine's Expository Dictionary of New Testament Words.* Like many Bible dictionaries, several reputable publishers print versions of this venerable work. Vine's provides detailed explanations and examples of usage for every Greek word in the New Testament. You'll uncover nuances and meanings that make the Bible come alive in new ways.

A Bible commentary: Such as the two volume *Bible Knowledge Commentary,* (Wheaton: Victor Books, 1983). Commentaries provide good explanations of books, chapters, and individual verses. Teens should remember that the content of any commentary, to one degree or another, will incorporate the author's own bias. This is not necessarily a bad thing, just something to keep in mind. Rather than taking everything at face value, we must always keep going back to Scripture, and should judge man's words in light of God's Word.

An interlinear New Testament: You probably already know that an interlinear Bible puts the original language text on the page right underneath the English words. You can look at the New Testament words and see a numbered Greek word right alongside its translated counterpart. Flip to the lexicon in the back, and *voila*: mucho info about each specific word that makes up our New Testament! An interlinear New Testament can look pretty intimidating at first glance, and I'll admit that many of your teens may not want to get into their Bible to this level. But these books can be navigated fairly painlessly and are quite helpful.

A "history of Christianity" book: Allow me to recommend three wonderful church history books. Each of these contains a wealth of information that is helpful to understanding the Bible. The following books are each a great read in their own right, they are not expensive, and I wish your teens would own them all. They are: *The 5-Minute Church Historian*, by Rick Cornish and Bruce Shelley (Navpress, 2005); *The Complete Book of When and Where in the Bible*, by E. Michael Rusten and Sharon Rusten (Tyndale, 2005); and *Christianity Through the Centuries*, by Earle Cairns (Zondervan, 1996).

Apologetics books: Knowledge of apologetics—*why* we believe *what* we believe—is mandatory for Christians today. My own book *STAND: Core Truths You Must Know For An Unshakable Faith* (Tyndale, 2005) is written at a seventh-grade reading level, explains the six most important themes of the Bible, and gives reasons why we hold them. The "magnum opus" of apologetics content is *The Baker Encyclopedia of Apologetics,* by Norman L. Geisler. This one-volume work covers every imaginable issue related to apologetics and defense of the biblical worldview.

While it is true that I lean toward the "hard copies" for serious study—books, research journals, and lots of my own scribbled-up legal pads—I don't want to minimize the use of resources that are online. An exhaustive listing of internet Bible study sites is, of course, impossible. But here are a few URL's that I especially recommend:

www.bible.org

www.biblegateway.com

www.ntcanon.org

www.scriptures.com

www.earlychristianwritings.com

www.inerrancy.com

BIBLICAL HERMENEUTICS: PRINCIPLES OF INTERPRETATION

Your students will ask about some problem areas—apparent contradictions or inconsistencies or difficult-to-understand passages.[15] One good general rule is that if it makes sense using common sense, don't twist it into nonsense. When a literal meaning works, use it.

Jesus never sought a hidden or secondary meaning when interpreting the Old Testament Scriptures. On the contrary, He consistently interpreted the Old Testament quite literally, including the Creation account of Adam and Eve (Matt. 13:35; 25:34; Mark 10:6), Noah's Ark and the Flood (Matt. 24:38-39; Luke 17:26-27), Jonah and the whale (Matt. 12:39-41), Sodom and Gomorrah (Matt. 10:15), and the account of Lot and his wife (Luke 17:28-29)[16]

Baker's Dictionary of Theology sums up a solid hermeneutical approach, advising us that the Bible should be interpreted literally, according to typical rules of grammar, within its historical context, and one passage cannot be interpreted in a way that conflicts with other passages.[17] When difficulties arise, there are three words that can solve many interpretational dilemmas. These are: *context, colloquial,* and *comprehensive.* Here's what I mean...

Context: Looking at the Larger Setting

A sure way to come to a hasty conclusion is to pull one verse out of context. For example, the Bible says, "There is no God." But Psalm 14:1 actually says, "The fool has said in his heart, 'There is no God.'" Most critics like to supposedly create a moral or ethical dilemma regarding things the Bible records by ignoring context. Nothing in Scripture contradicts itself. Show your students that cults frequently pull Scripture out of context and create doctrines out of it. You will only end in error if you base a teaching on an obscure passage, where meaning is not always clear.

Reading in context generally means, at a minimum, reading both the chapter before and the one after the chapter you are studying. Remember also to interpret difficult passages in the light of clear ones in other chapters or books of the Bible. Even the use of specific words can be compared for clarity. "To ascertain the meaning of a word or passage, it is very frequently of the greatest importance to study parallel passages. What is obscure or doubtful in one passage is often clear in another; or one passage may throw light on another."[18]

Colloquialisms: Understanding Figures of Speech

We must also remember that God used the peculiarities of speech, personalities, and culture of His pen men. An agrarian culture should not be expected to speak in the same terms as our informational and scientific age. If a passage is not intended to have precision, it is not an error when precision by our standards is not found. The truthfulness of Scripture is not negated by either irregularities of grammar or spelling, or seeming discrepancies between two passages.[19] None of these minor differences affect any of the doctrines. The Bible also includes a variety of genre, or types of writing: history, law, poetry, prophecy, hyperbole, metaphors, narratives, and epistles (letters or correspondence with a godly message to the recipients). Thus, a metaphor would obviously be interpreted figuratively, and letters might not necessarily present events in chronological order.

If a literal translation does not make normal sense, the writer is probably using some figure of speech. Jesus often spoke in parables. When He said, "I am the door" (John 10:9), we know He didn't literally mean He was a wooden object leading into a room. When Scripture speaks of God having wings, from all we know about God from the Bible, it does not mean He literally has physical wings. Symbolic language has its place in the Bible, as it does in other pieces of literature.

Comprehensive: Keep the Overall Message in Mind

Keep in mind that the overall message of the Bible is salvation through God's Son, Jesus Christ.[20] Look at the whole panorama or message of God's revelation through this truth. Apologist Hank Hanegraaff often says that the Old Testament is the "background music" playing as you read the New Testament. The Bible's consistent harmonization with itself is amazing and beautiful. The comprehensive theme is: "God's Son, and how you may know Him." The sixty-six books of the Bible were written by forty human agents specifically chosen by God, spanning 1,600-2,000 years, with one common theme running throughout—the Messiah, Jesus Christ. No one but God could give us such a unified, powerful book. The Bible is not a haphazard collection of books.

TYING IT ALL TOGETHER

One of my favorite verses in all of Scripture is Psalm 119:93 (NLT), which says, "I will never forget your commandments, for by them you give me life." Clearly, the Bible is vital to both salvation and Christian growth. Because we are not called merely to be *converts* but *disciples,* study of God's Word is an inseparable part of a consistent Christian life. There are eight basic things to keep in mind as you approach God's Word. The Bible is faithfully handled when read (1) prayerfully; (2) reverently; (3) personally; (4) contextually; (5) textually; (6) applicably; (7) consistently; and (8) obediently. Again, remember that, "When the Scripture makes clear sense, seek no other sense, or you will have nonsense."

Remind teens that the Bible is a priceless roadmap for decision-making and godly living. (What does the text say? What is my responsibility in light of what the text says?) God's Word should guide our beliefs, our behavior, and our worship. With a commitment to these eight basics, your students' lives will be transformed.

REVIEW QUESTIONS

1. What are some proofs that the Bible has been accurately passed down to us and is reliable?

2. Why is it important to know that the Bible is authentic?

3. What is your biggest challenge in having a Bible study and prayer time each day?

4. If you cannot afford to buy any Bible study resources, what are other ways you can access them?

5. Using principles of hermeneutics, what are some contradictory passages that you can now resolve?

6. What are some everyday examples of a change in meaning when statements are pulled out of context?

CHAPTER 6

Get to the Point:
Communicating Biblical Truth to Students

I was so excited because I was going to get to preach in "big church." Yes, I was going to preach to adults during a real worship service. Halfway through the message I noticed that no one was listening. I was boring, and I could tell by the blank stares and by those looking out of the windows that I wasn't communicating anything.

How does one communicate what God has put in his heart? There may be nothing wrong with the message but usually it is the technique by which one communicates that has gone awry. I am sharing in this chapter the things I have learned over thirty years of speaking that have given success in getting the message from my heart to the hearts of others. It is simple and it works!

THE PROPOSITIONAL STATEMENT, OR WHAT AM I TRYING TO SAY?

As I study through a passage of Scripture and some truth hits my heart and begins to change me I want to share it with others. So I picture myself standing in front of an audience ready to speak and then I ask myself, "What are you trying to say?"

That's why a speaker needs a propositional statement. What idea am I proposing? If I can take my message or idea and put it into one sentence, then I know what I am going to talk about. The biggest problem for many speakers is that they have some idea or "warm fuzzy feeling" about a passage, but it isn't a complete idea or principle that they really understand. If the speaker doesn't understand it, the audience surely won't get it either.

A propositional statement is that basic foundation which the speaker will build on for the whole message. It is a capsule of the whole message. It is that which the speaker will use to transition from point to point and give the listener guidance through the message (and hope that it will come to an end).

There are five elements of a propositional statement. They are: number, noun, complement (or purpose), application, and it should be written in twelve words or less.

The best way for me to show you how to develop a propositional statement and to illustrate all eight of the principles that I will share about structuring a message is to actually walk you through a message and show you how I would do it. I am choosing the story of David and Goliath from 1 Samuel 17.

You are probably familiar with the story David and Goliath. David, a teenage shepherd fights a champion warrior, Goliath, who is also a giant. David succeeds in defeating the giant Goliath. Now how could a young boy overcome an experienced man of war? Was it luck or did David possess great character to meet the challenge of the day? I *propose* to you that it was character!

Where did David receive this "character" to defeat the giant? I *propose* to you that he developed it when he was a shepherd. How do I know that? I read it in 1 Samuel 17: 31-37. The key to the victory is revealed from this conversation between David and King Saul. David convinces Saul to let him fight the giant because of three qualities of character he received while being a shepherd.

Therefore, my propositional statement is: "Three Character Qualities You Need to be a Giant-Killer for God." Let's look at the five elements of our propositional statement:

Number: "Three."

Noun: "Character Qualities."

Complement (or purpose): "To be a giant-killer for God."

Application: "You need."

Twelve words or less: (the statement is only twelve words).

I can work off of this propositional statement through my whole message. It guides me as to what I want to say, how much I want to say, to whom, and for what reason.

A propositional statement is much more than a title. A title just gives you the *noun* but not the purpose of why you are talking about the noun and what it will do for the listener.

It reminds me of a time when I was visiting a church at Christmas time and the pastor's sermon title on the bulletin was "A Christmas Passage." What about the passage? What am I supposed to do about the passage? Is there application for my life or are we just going to observe a passage about Christmas and then gain some knowledge and go home?

So as you study a passage ask yourself, "What am I trying to say?" Make sure there is a complement or purpose to what you are saying. Always put the listener in the center of the message. This message is not just to learn about the Bible, it is to learn about what the Bible says that will change his life—that's the application!

USE INSTRUCTIONAL POINTS.

When I was a young Christian, I always wondered about the difference between an interesting message and a boring message. I was on my own journey of learning to speak and I listened to speakers with similar educational backgrounds and beliefs but found that some could hold my interest and inspire me, while others were boring and I would find my mind wandering. What is the secret to exciting communication?

Well, one of the first things that I discovered about being a good speaker is to use instructional points. One of the great preachers of old that I used to read was Charles Spurgeon. I would get so excited reading his messages (and he was dead)! So what was in the body of his messages that was keeping me interested when, quite frankly, many messages I heard audibly were boring? As I studied his written messages I noticed that his points were instructional.

What do I mean by *instructional*? In other words, when you are speaking, give the people something to do! How many sermons have I heard where the preacher's points are just statements. Take for instance the passage we are looking at about David and Goliath in 1 Samuel 17. If I am just going to preach an accurate outline of the activity that happens here, I would give it a lame title: *David and Goliath*. Then I would have outline points such as: 1) David takes provisions to his brothers; 2) David talks to Saul; 3) David was a shepherd; 4) David kills the giant. *So what?*

Just because I properly outline a passage doesn't mean that I have helped anybody live the Christian life better. But, if you look for the true message of the passage and instruct people what to do with this truth, you will keep them engaged in your message. Give them something to do with the truth. Don't just state facts.

When I preach 1 Samuel 17:31-37, I try to see how I can instruct others to be like David. These verses have to do with David's conversation with Saul. Saul asks David why he is willing and able to fight the giant Goliath. David gives Saul his resume. He says that as he kept his father's sheep, a lion took one and David went after the lion, killed it, and rescued the sheep. I noticed that nobody was looking, except God. So, to put the first point (or first *character quality* from my propositional statement) as an instructional point, I write: 1) Do what's right when you are alone.

Do you see how point one is instructional? You can do that when you go home. You can be just like David. At this moment, I am not just interested in seeing what David did; I am interested in getting my listeners to follow David in character quality.

As the passage progresses, I see that David says that he killed a lion and a bear. Wow, they are big things! So the next point (or character quality) is: 2) Face extreme difficulties over and over.

Do you see how point two is instructional? Your audience can do that when they go home. The next point is also instructional. I read that David says that God delivered him from the lion and bear and will deliver him from the giant. My third point is simply: 3) Ask God for help. Can the listener do that when he goes home? Yes, and he can do that sitting right there, beginning immediately. Give the people something to do! I state the points of my messages instructionally. It keeps your listeners involved and they feel challenged to action.

EXPLAIN YOUR POINTS.

After I have chosen my points and made them instructional, they must be explained. This is when one is really teaching. The instructional point is simply a brief synopsis of what you are going to teach about a part of the passage. It is a continuation of the propositional statement in the sense of explaining in depth what you are talking about.

The instructional point is simply a brief synopsis of what you are going to teach about a part of the passage

Let's go back to our passage in 1 Samuel 17:31-37. The first point (Do what's right when you are alone), referring back to the propositional statement (Three Character Qualities You Need to be a Giant-Killer for God), now needs to be *explained*. In other words, what does it mean when you say, "Do what's right when you are alone"?

Here's what I mean by "Do what's right when you are alone." After I have read the Scripture passage, given the propositional statement, and then given my first point, I explain: The true measure of a person is what they do when they are alone! You elongate the meaning of the point so that people will get the principle of life you are trying to teach.

Of course, I certainly go back to the Scripture and explain where I got the principle. I would point out that David was all alone as a shepherd boy. No one was watching him. One day a lion comes and takes a lamb out of the flock and starts to carry it off. David responsibly goes after the lion, takes the lamb from it, and kills the lion. He doesn't do the *right thing* because a crowd is cheering for him or because he will be recognized as a great hero. He doesn't do it for his own convenience, ease, comfort, or safety. He fights the lion because he is a shepherd, and shepherds are supposed to guard the sheep, and his father has given him this responsibility—and God is watching (we aren't really alone)!

What great character David had, I explain, to put his life on the line for a lamb. No other person was watching, but David did what was right when he was alone. God was watching though, and He was looking for a king to replace the failed kingdom of Saul. It does matter what one does when he or she is alone. It was no mistake that God asked David to bring bread to his brothers in the army so that he would be present to fight the giant. David had passed the test of courage and responsibility when he was alone and now God was going to use him to be a giant-killer.

Points are great if they are instructional, but you see how they must be explained. The points are the bones of the outline and the explanation for every point is the "meat on the bones."

FIND PARALLEL ILLUSTRATIONS TO YOUR POINTS.

Another very important part of an instructional outline is to illustrate each point. Over the years of speaking I have learned the importance of illustrating the truth that I am talking about.

Each point of your speech has a principle of truth behind it. A good

A good illustration will give the listener a parallel picture of the truth you are teaching.

illustration will give the listener a parallel picture of the truth you are teaching. I believe that there are five dimensions to an illustration.

An illustration:

1. Is a parallel *picture* of the principle truth of the point. It creates a bird's-eye view of the point. This picture encapsulates the truth.

2. Is a story about the principle that allows the mind to *rest*. It is easy to listen to a story after the mind has been taxed with comprehending the principle of the point.

3. Is a way to *remember* the principle being taught. Illustrations are "hooks" to hang our memory upon. Long after the listener has forgotten the title of your point he will still remember the illustration that portrayed the point.

4. Is a way to *clarify* the truth that you are teaching. What good is a lesson that is brilliant but has left the listener in a fog because he just didn't get it!

5. Is an avenue for the listener to *comprehend quickly*. There is a limited amount of time for each point and then the speaker must move on to the next one. Illustrations are shortcuts to understanding.

Let me take you back now to 1 Samuel 17 and the sample sermon. As I give point one and explain it, the listeners' minds are trying to absorb all of the meaning of what I am saying. So I interject an illustration after the explanation to help the listener to grasp what it means to do right when he's alone.

Here's a sample illustration to consider. Suppose you get a job at a fast-food restaurant flipping hamburgers. You accidentally sneeze on one, but wrap it and send it to the customer anyhow (a responsible employee would have fried another hamburger for the customer's sake). The customer remarks that he didn't ask for relish on his hamburger, but you irresponsibly say, "Oh, just scrape it off." Then you joke with your friends later about how funny it was.

Here's the point of the illustration. Because you were flipping hamburgers alone and nobody saw you sneeze on the hamburger, there were no consequences—or were there? Nobody saw but God, and that's Who counts. Did you do what was right when you were alone? No! Were you like David? No! Did God see? Yes! Will you get promoted? Maybe, but not by God. God promoted David, but He probably won't promote you because you don't do right when you are alone.

Illustrations accomplish the five dimensions I mentioned above. Can you see how this simple parable about flipping hamburgers fulfilled all five concerning the principle of the point, "Do what's right when you are alone." Believe me, illustrations are very important, especially in the visual culture we live in today. So make sure that each point is supported with a fitting illustration.

APPLICATION: APPLY EACH POINT.

As I use my propositional statement to move through each instructional point, I make sure that I explain each point, illustrate each point, and now I am ready to apply what I have taught from this point. Application is so important because it brings your listeners to a decision. If you have been presenting instructional points and given the people something to do, then you can challenge them as to what they are going to do with the lesson you just taught.

Application is the most neglected element of teaching or of speaking today. It does little good to give lots of correct, good information and theologically correct and orthodox (proper interpretation) information about the Bible, if you don't ask your audience to do anything with this information. In other words, "What about you? What are you going to do about this information?"

Let's return to the lesson we are putting together about David from 1 Samuel 17:31-37. The propositional statement helps us know that we are trying to acquire character qualities that will make us capable of overcoming giant problems in the name of God. Point one instructs the listener to do what is right when he is alone. You have explained what this means and illustrated this principle so that he can understand clearly and quickly. Now comes the big question (application): "Listener, what do *you* do when you are alone?"

This message isn't just information about a shepherd boy who stood for God and was able to kill a giant. This message is for the benefit of every listener!! This is not about David, it is about *you*!

A good illustration concerning application is the account of the Prophet Nathan who confronted King David about his sin of adultery and murder. Nathan presented a lesson through a story of a poor man with one sheep and a rich man with many sheep who killed the poor man and took his one sheep. The message got through to David as a great injustice. He saw the principle and shouted out that the rich man should pay for his sin. Nathan the prophet then looked at the king and declares, "*You* are the man!" Ah, application.

Most lessons or sermons today have nothing for the listener to apply. When I speak, I want my audience to have something to do and I challenge them with application to their lives. If I am preaching about David doing right when he was alone, then that is just the stage to ask the people if they are going to do right when they are alone.

I might apply point one in this way: "What do you do when you are alone? What do *you* do when your parents leave to go to the store and you are home alone? Do you watch improper shows on TV when no one is watching you? Do you work hard and honestly at your job when your employer is not watching you? Do you steal when no one is watching? Do you cheat when no one is watching?"

If I apply the message to each one's life in the audience, then they have something to do. They may have something to clean up in their lives. The listener is not just thinking about David's journey to great character quality, he is thinking about his own life and what he needs to do personally if he is going to become a "giant-killer" for God.

By the way, application happens at the end of each instructional point. Some speakers like to do it at the very end of the message, but I think it is more effective at each point because I believe the listener can forget the points' application if I wait to the very end. For instance, at the end of point two (Face extreme difficulties), I would apply this point by asking, "Do you face tough circumstances or run away from them? What is waiting for you back home that you need to face?" And for the third point (Ask God for help), I could ask, "Do you need to ask God to help you right now?"

If there is no application, then there is no call to action. If there is application, then I can invite the listener to decision. Some ask me why students respond to my messages when I give an invitation or altar call. I tell them that it is the fact that I gave them something to do (instructional points) and then I applied the truth of the Scriptures to their twenty-first century lives and asked them to make a decision. That's application!

If there is no application, then there is no call to action.

INTERACT WITH YOUR AUDIENCE.

The cry of the education community today is, "No child left behind!" That comes from a desire to see each student understand the material of the curriculum of his or her age group and graduate with a grasp of the material. Hopefully no one drops out of school along the way because he or she just didn't get it or got bored. Well, that is my goal for each message I preach or each lesson I teach. No listener gets left behind!

Did you ever notice while listening to a speaker that no one is paying attention? I sometimes look around the room after I have become bored during a lecture and have lost the speaker's train of thought to see if others have checked out. There are a lot of blank stares on faces and the listeners seem to be politely sitting there just waiting for the droning noise of someone's voice to stop. There is no understanding and total boredom. Why?

I believe that a speaker that may have a great message from his heart sometimes doesn't get it through to other hearts because he has left the listeners behind. I personally notice when my audience gets bored or tired of listening and it is time to get them back. Please try to learn the skill of noticing boredom in your audience. Don't just plow ahead to get this thing over with. That's what I sense a lot of speakers do.

How do I get my listeners to listen? Well, that's what I call *interaction!* The speaker needs to interact with his audience all through his speech. It is simple and yet a very challenging skill to develop as a speaker. I had to learn it over the years and it is a very useful tool in the art of communicating to a crowd.

What do I mean by interaction? It is literally carrying on a conversation with the audience through your whole message. It is definitely not lecturing. I want the crowd involved and interacting with me so that they won't go to sleep as I speak.

How do I interact with a crowd as I speak? I use rhetorical questions. I move around so that people have to follow me with their eyes and not just their minds and ears. I will laugh at my own grammatical mistakes and pause to correct them, perhaps asking the audience the proper way to say something. These are all ways to leave no listener behind.

It has been my experience that most audiences, especially in church settings, are not used to following the speaker. They have been trained that when the speaker starts, to simply check out! That's why interaction is an art form and must be developed. Be determined to leave no listener behind! The Word of God is not boring and we, too, who proclaim the Word of God should not be boring!

EARNESTNESS: BE PASSIONATE ABOUT THE TRUTH.

As I was learning how to be an effective speaker, one of the most important things I ever learned about communicating the Word of God was to be earnest, passionate, or excited as I spoke. Truth is exciting but sometimes our demeanor in delivering the truth communicates something different.

I was reading a message by Charles Haddon Spurgeon (a preacher in London in the nineteenth century) one day with the purpose of helping young men learn how to preach effective "soul-winning" sermons. One of his points was to be earnest. *Earnest* is an old word that we seldom use today, but it means to be passionate, or what we might even say in Christian vernacular: "to be on fire." If the truth is exciting, then it ought to touch our hearts in a way before we preach it that would set our speech on fire as we do speak it.

The illustration that Spurgeon gave in his message is one that I will never forget. It was an illustration about a neighbor's house on fire. The story was of a house on fire and a neighbor who goes to warn the occupants of the house on fire to get out. The neighbor slovenly and delicately tosses pebbles at the window to wake the residents to warn them of their danger. Those inside the house finally respond to the faint plink of tiny stones upon their window. The neighbor politely informs them of the truth of their dilemma that their house is on fire. The man at the window promptly dumps water on the neighbor's head for bothering them. If the house was truly on fire the man in the house surmises that his neighbor would have said it in an entirely different and earnestly excited way!

Wow! It clicked with me at that time of my young speaking career that I did not speak with passion. I wasn't earnest with the truth when I spoke to people. I simply stated the truth and let what may happen, happen. I knew I had to start speaking with passion and with earnestness if I was going to touch hearts in an effective way. Just like the neighbor who was unconvincing about stating the truth of the house on fire in a matter-of-fact way, I, too, had been guilty of understating the exciting truths of the Gospel dispassionately.

I remember getting up to speak after learning this principle. What a difference it made in the audience. They seemed to be interested and excited about what I was speaking about and I even heard a few "amen's." It also made me aware of the condition of my own heart as I spoke. I had to honestly ask myself if I was excited enough about the truth I was preaching to be passionate in my delivery. I also remember people asking me as they exited the church, "What happened to you?" They had noticed a difference but probably didn't understand that it was simply a man preaching with conviction and passion. I believed it and preached like it!

There are a few things that must be kept in mind as passion is added to a message. First, I never want to fake a passion about the truth. If it hasn't really impacted my heart, I don't try to drum up some kind of excitement. People will know anyway. They will sense sincerity or falsehood when it involves earnestness and passion. Second, I don't want to speak *only* with passion. Inflection with the tone of voice is very important as one speaks. A speaker who starts off at a high, excited pitch and stays there throughout the whole message will exhaust his listeners. Passion is effective when it is used at the proper place of a message. I want to use passion to emphasize the most important points and applications of my message.

SUMMARY

As I create a message, I want to ask myself, "What are you trying to say?" When I figure that out, I put that idea into a propositional statement. I work from the propositional statement throughout my message, using it to transition from one point to the next until I am done; then I review the propositional statement as a summary of what I have spoken.

I choose instructional points that support the idea of my propositional statement. The instructional points give the people to whom I am speaking something to do. I explain the principle of each point, illustrate each point, and then apply each point.

As I preach using the above methods, I keep my audience awake and alert by interacting with them through subtle rhetorical questions. I also make sure that I believe what I am saying and speak the truth with passion because I have the greatest message in the world: the Gospel of Jesus Christ.

REVIEW QUESTIONS

1. What are the five elements of a propositional statement?
2. What is the difference between a propositional statement and a title?
3. What is the question speakers should always ask themselves as they develop a message, devotion, or speech?
4. How does a propositional statement help the speaker throughout the message?
5. What are the five dimensions of an illustration and what do each of these dimensions accomplish through the illustration?
6. What is the crucial reason for the application?

CHAPTER 7

Finding Common Ground:
Making Intergenerational Connections

Okay, this may sound like an oxymoron (intergenerational youth ministry) but think about what could be more normal than other generations being a part of ministry to today's students? I'm not trying to get back to "back in the day" days, nor am I trying to sound culturally relevant (even though anyone who knows anything about youth ministry knows that being culturally relevant is a youth ministry mantra). So let's sound culturally relevant while suggesting some "back in the day" common sense.

COME TO TERMS

Intergenerational ministry has been defined as "transformational relationships: connecting elders and young people and all ages in-between; finding common ground, mutual interests, and places where we 'fill each others' gaps'; building a warm, healthy community. Sometimes, these things can only happen by intentionally creating the appropriate conditions. Other times, it is simply a matter of intentionally recognizing the possibilities in an existing environment."[1] Angie Clark defines it this way: "Intergenerational ministry is ministry that criss crosses generational lines. It is allowing for ministry of 1) children to adults, 2) teens to children, 3) children to teens, 4) teens to adults in addition to the usual, adult to teens or adult to children. It is not only allowing this kind of interaction, but encouraging it and giving opportunity for it within the church structure at as many levels/ministries as possible."[2]

Contrary to these definitions, many churches tend to segregate the generations, from teenagers to children. Now I would be the first proponent to that kind of ministry segregation. It should be done and done well. But within those segregated groups, other generations need to be integrated into leadership and as participants. On the flip side, there needs to be ministry that includes a coming together of the generations:

> Other church analysts and church leaders are seriously questioning age-specific ministries in at least two ways. First, rising evidence shows that ministries that are not intergenerational may not be as pragmatically valuable as they first seem. Recent studies by George Barna and Mark DeVries argue that the short-term gains received through age-specific ministries are not consistent over the long haul. Their separate studies indicate that young people raised in age-specific ministries often don't remain in the church after they become adults. Likewise, people who attend age-specific congregations tend to stop attending church altogether when they "outgrow" their current church.[3]

Mark DeVries says it even more succinctly:

> Are we connecting our kids to nurturing relationships that will last them after they complete their teenage years, or are we simply exploiting them as public relations tools to make our ministries appear successful? I submit that unless we are making intentional, focused efforts at connecting kids with mature Christian adults in the church (not just their youth leaders), we are more like the vultures preying on kids at rock concerts and less like the spiritual leaders praying that their children's lives would be founded upon eternal things.[4]

So somewhere along the way, some purposeful merging of the generations needs to take place, usually in some main church gathering or service. When it comes to "big church," leadership needs to strive toward having parts of the service, from time to time, "speak" to their younger generations. Something that is said or done or performed or sung needs to catch the attention of the younger, more scrutinizing audience, no matter how minimal it may be. Something needs to resonate with this younger generation, something that they recognize. If you attempt this, there may be a "rub" with some folks. So be prepared.

FOCUS ON THE FAMILY

Some common sensibility to inter-generational youth ministry has to include the importance of family. Moms and dads, uncles and aunts, cousins, grandparents — you name it — everyone has an important role and should embrace it, whether it be for a moment or a season or a lifetime. Now don't get me wrong, many of us do embrace these roles with enthusiasm. But culture has made this considerably more difficult. Take mobility: we are everywhere and we go everywhere. Why? Because we can! In many situations, employment determines where we go and what we do. The down side of this is the distance we've put between the ones we usually trust the most — family.

I am no one to talk here. When Pam and I married, we moved from Florida to southern California. My family was in Florida and her family was in Wisconsin. Now when there are no kids in the picture, this isn't a bad idea. It was just the two of us, no in-laws to run to, just each other. But when kids entered the picture, the absence of extended family became more noticeable. And of all places, I decided to move to Edmonton, Alberta in Canada—another country! Now we did all we could to remain connected, but three thousand mile (one way) road trips got real old real quick (and expensive). So involvement and influence from extended family members was sporadic at best. Whether it's three thousand miles or three hundred, family has been distanced from each other. So anything that comes close to a facsimile of family members is always a good thing.

On the youth ministry side of things, intergenerational means including as much family as possible.

On the youth ministry side of things, intergenerational means including as much family as possible. I don't mean necessarily doing stuff where the entire family is welcome. I know there have been some good "college tries" here but frankly, sometimes young people need their space as well as their place to simply be teenagers. But I am saying that having parental and grandparental types, who are best described as matriarchal and patriarchal in their demeanor, would go far in effectual ministry among young people. Their involvement can be regular or seasonal. But whatever the involvement, it is needed and should be wanted.

REAL AGE

Now let's be honest: in most church youth ministries, age and maturity are not always top on the priority list of desirable characteristics. It can sometimes be described as more of "young and dumb." This needs to change. It does not have to be one or the other. It really should be a combination of the two. Youth ministries need the age, maturity, experience, wisdom, and resources of an older generation. Youth ministries paradoxically need the youthfulness, enthusiasm, energy, technical savvy, and entrepreneurial spirit of a younger generational leader.

Youth ministries need the age, maturity, experience, wisdom, and resources of an older generation.

Now let me get something off my chest: age is relative and age is unavoidable. Some people are old because they think in old ways. Their age of mentality has caught up with their chronological age. If you begin to think old (or in old ways), then you are old, no matter what chronological age you are.[5]

I work in a very fast-paced Christian university (Liberty University). Before his death, the founder of the school, Dr. Jerry Falwell, was chronologically an older man (seventies). But if you hung around him long enough, you knew that he did not think old. Things progressed, ideas were exchanged, decisions were made, decisions changed, initiative was encouraged, visions came to fruition...everything was kept on track and on message, as a direct result of his tutelage and his age-less thinking.

He was the quintessential example of a patriarch who did not think old and had an effectual ministry among young college students. Maybe you've met "him" before (no, not Dr. Falwell). I am talking about the person who is in your church or ministry. There aren't many of them but when you have them, you wish you had a dozen more like them.

Richard Sherwin was on my board of directors with Youth for Christ. He was always thinking of ways to do business so he could make more money to help financially support our ministry (when you're in the support raising ministry, you really love guys like this). He was fast-moving, not afraid to ask, not afraid to give, not afraid to interrupt, not afraid to take a risk, and not afraid to identify with a ministry to teenagers and help make things happen. And he was well into his seventies, playing golf, body surfing, and deal-making, when he was overtaken by a debilitating and eventually fatal stroke. That one hurt. He was always a source of encouragement. The glass was always half full with Richard.

AN EASY BUTTON

Okay, you're probably looking for the "handle" to make this an easy step toward intergenerational leadership. That's what I'd be looking for. This is where I'd be using my highlighter. To make it attractive for other generations to be involved in youth ministry, you have to make it easy for them. In even more simple words, you need to create ministry situations that make it easy for older generations to interact and minister to the young generation. Let's face it. Teenagers can be a bit intimidating. Thanks to the

...you need to create ministry situations that make it easy for older generations to interact and minister to the young generation.

Internet, they are the most intelligent and most impatient generation ever. (it takes Google .11 seconds to find 126,000,000 sites for MTV. Really? It takes that long?!) So who wouldn't be intimidated?

Let me give you an example of "easy." Many ministries are now investing in youth ministry via the development and construction of youth rooms and youth centers. Kind of like a community center with a spiritual dynamic integrated into the program. Sometimes these facilities are in the current church building, or a separate building on the property, or a free-standing structure off the property. But a youth center is a way to making it easy for other generations to be involved. Why? You just show up! "Oh yeah, stand over there and play a game with a teenager."

In one youth center I was in, the entire youth center was designed for interaction. There were no snack machines or soda machines. You had to ask an adult for something to eat or drink. All the games were designed for interaction, in that you had to play against someone, usually an adult. So what's hard about that? Stand there and play. Now that's easy. The kids come to you! Not so threatening. That is what has to be developed: ministry situations where the students have to come to you to engage, to interact, to talk; situations where it's adults that need to be sought out, where adults are in positions of leadership.

I was in one church in Tipp City, Ohio (near Dayton) where the church invested in a youth center (The Avenue) on the church property. The attendance of teenagers in the area was overwhelming. I met a retired individual who became the "go to" person for all the skaters that were coming. Retired guys tend to know how to fix things. They may not know skateboard linguistics (decks, ramps, rails, grind rails, etc.) but given a little time, they can figure it out. So this retiree got to know a bunch of middle school students who were all about skateboarding, and loved this man, no matter what his age was. Who knows? Maybe he was a surrogate father or grandfather to a bunch of young teenage boys who needed him in that role.

A COUPLE OF THINGS TO THINK ABOUT

For a more traditional approach to purposeful placement of older generations in youth ministry, there are some other factors to consider. First, you have to take into consideration a person's spiritual gifts, personal skills, and personality. Some would say that spiritual gifts trump personal skills and personality. I would disagree. All three must be considered even if one may be more prominent than the other. This may be a bit subjective, as far as your own judgment here. Probably your best ally is time: time to see how they are doing, the reaction of students, and the gaining of rapport (or lack of) with those students. Are they comfortable around students? Are students comfortable around them?

...you have to take into consideration a person's spiritual gifts, personal skills, and personality.

A second factor would be permission, specifically from parents. Okay, another highlight statement is coming. Not all parents are automatically qualified to be involved with your youth ministry, simply because they have teenagers (or were once teenagers themselves). You know whom I'm talking about. They're kind of like pseudo teenagers, either reliving their own adolescent years or they are living their adolescent years vicariously through their own teenagers. Here is a "trick of the trade" in youth ministry. Have parents get permission from their own teenagers to work in their youth ministry. That's right, parents get permission. Either their teenagers won't mind, or there is no way during this lifetime that will happen, or involvement will be conditional. Those conditions will vary from a limited amount of time, to a trial basis. By the way, anyone involved among your students should be on a trial basis.

PROGRAMMING IS NOT A BAD WORD

A discussion of intergenerational leadership in youth ministry must factor in the issue of programming if we are to consider the entire equation. Programming for some is a bad word. It seems too calculated, not spontaneous. It is perceived as not having much guidance from the Holy Spirit. Some see it as heavy on human input and light on spiritual insight. Youth ministry is spontaneous by nature and often spontaneity is equated with the leading of the Holy Spirit. I would suggest that this spontaneity can be experienced in youth ministry programming, giving thought and structure before plans are carried out, while allowing the freedom to change it up or even abandoning plans, when appropriate.

In the meantime, I think it would be foolish to think that if I just let things fall into place, without giving leadership and thoughtful direction, then everything will work out. Of course there needs to be room for a bit of entrepreneurial and cavalier thinking. But it would be difficult to maintain the confidence of parents and adults if this was a consistent and regular modus operandi. Instead, we should consider Holy Spirit-leading, while we plan and program. So within that framework, we allow elbow room to experience things that weren't necessarily planned or programmed, while maintaining some resemblance of structure and knowledge of what is supposed to take place.

WHAT TO LOOK FOR IN INTERGENERATIONAL LEADERSHIP

Many times when intergenerational youth ministry is considered, what we are really asking is, "Where can I get some adults to run small groups, teach a particular class, and so forth?" Again, we need to make this as relatively easy as possible. Not everyone is cut out for teaching, though they can be trained. But the teaching, mentoring, discipleship role is typically a paramount need. One key thing not to do is advertise.

Putting a "Want Ad" on your website or church bulletin is not the best of ideas. Instead, identify potential intergenerational leaders. Pray for wisdom and discernment here and don't go it alone. Lean on the Holy Spirit's guidance and spiritual

Putting a "Want Ad" on your website or church bulletin is not the best of ideas.

advisors. After that, it's time to let them know of the need and to give consideration to your leadership needs. Let me make some suggestions as to what kind of person to look for:

* easily gains rapport with teenagers

* pretty good reader of personalities (among teenagers)

* sensitive to teenagers' individual learning styles

* comfortable with their own age

* not easily agitated

* strives toward a leadership style of servanthood

* an ability to listen

* teenagers feel safe around them

* able to forecast potential problems

* recognize varying levels of spiritual development among teenagers

* open to partnerships with other intergenerational leaders

* not quick to judge

* spontaneity and a sense of humor are always a plus

* willingness to take directions as well as confident to make suggestions

* whether they are a parent or not, they need think like a parent

* their personal faith is growing and transparent

I know what you're thinking: "in a perfect world...maybe." This is an ambitious list. So will you get the entire package in every potential leader? Probably not, but you need to see a combination of these suggestions. For any deficiencies, spell out your expectations. Most misunderstandings in this type of ministry relationship result from not knowing expectations, so spell them out. The previous list of suggestions would make a pretty good list of expectations. This will go a long way in building a team of intergenerational leaders for your youth ministry.

For any deficiencies, spell out your expectations.

With the need for teaching, mentoring, or discipleship, let's go back to "easy." The most valuable commodity that adults have is time (it used to be money but many adults would rather give money than time), so respect that. Your intergenerational leaders may not have the kind of time you have to develop and prepare material for discussion groups, teaching small groups, whatever. Provide them the tools and resources to do the kind of job you expect.

Provide them the tools and resources to do the kind of job you expect.

Another helpful tip is to give your leadership a start date and an end date (usually a school year). People are reluctant to get involved when there is no end date. Now that doesn't mean that they will only be involved for that year. Usually leaders stay on much longer. But at least they have the option. Another thing, give them the summer off (this is also beneficial to vocational youth leaders). Modify your ministry plans to accommodate this. Everyone needs a break and many times after a break, people are ready to get back into it, with a renewed vigor and enthusiasm.

BOYS WILL BE BOYS

I was watching a news story about animals. It seems that in Kruger National Park in Namibia, Africa, the game wardens had a baffling problem. Someone was poaching their white rhinoceros. Now poaching is obviously illegal. But what was confounding them was the fact that the poachers were leaving the entire animal. Typically, poachers harvest the tail, feet, and of course, the horn. But these carcasses were left to rot in the African sun. Besides the legalities, this simply didn't make any sense. Who would do such a thing?

Some of the game reserve officials had an idea: put up surveillance cameras in locations where the white rhinos would frequent, particularly watering holes, and see if they could capture on videotape the perpetrators. Several days passed and still no suspects or arrests, so the officials started reviewing the tapes. To their surprise, it wasn't poachers killing rhinos; it was orphaned adolescent bull elephants. The cruel irony is that these young bull elephants had their older male elephants poached. So in an animal planet sort of way, these young bull elephants had formed their own "gang."

Videotape captured them ganging up on white rhinoceros, antagonizing them by tossing logs, spraying water, and then surrounding them and stomping them to death. A fatal attraction of intimidation was taking place. There were no older bull elephants to put them in place, to keep them in check. So these adolescent bull elephants were virtually doing whatever they pleased, from harassing tourists to killing anything that stood in their way. Game officials came up with a novel idea: import older bull elephants. They did and the problem disappeared overnight. Older bulls told the younger bulls to "smarten up" and if they didn't, they were disciplined in an elephant sort of way.

So what is the analogy? We have a problem with our teenage guys. Many are out of control, without any direction or guidance from older males in their lives. So they go about their lives, intimidating, harassing, and hurting anyone in their way. There is a vacuum of older male adults to keep them in check.

There is a vacuum of older male adults to keep them in check.

Whether we like it or not, this sociological phenomenon will have a significant impact as to whom we will be ministering. If there ever was a critical mass in intergenerational youth ministry, this would be it. Now before you think I've abandoned the girls, I haven't. But let's be honest; girls tend to follow the leader. So without intentionally sounding a bit stereotypical, we need to address the guys. The problem is critical. Thousands of boys walk the streets with little support from the services of community, school, or even church.

It isn't until they become bad that they attract the interest of the criminal justice system. That is when they get any significant attention, but by that time, it may be too late. In his book *Angry Young Men*, Dr. Aaron Kipnis presents some sobering facts. Worst case scenario is the fact that adolescent guys are four to five times more "successful" in their suicide attempts (this is a bitter difference between the sexes: whereas girls tend to rationalize and become emotional, guys are more determined to carry out the threat). The Center for Disease Control (CDC) says that nearly twenty percent of all ninth to twelfth grade students periodically carry a weapon to school (the majority of them say it is because they feel threatened). Homicide is the second leading cause of death among young people between the ages of fifteen and twenty-four (ten times higher than Canada). Between five and fifteen million children of working parents are home alone after school. More than half of all juvenile crime occurs between two and eight p.m.

The ministry challenges are enormous. Where do we start? Let's start with ourselves. Dr. Kipnis explains that guys need to have a sense that you are cool. "What is cool? Being direct, courteous, at ease, authentic, egalitarian and most of all...your words come from your heart, and the actions you take demonstrate that no matter how challenging or novel your intervention may look, a bad boy can trust that every move is designed for his welfare, not his subversion."[7]

After that, it will take intergenerational youth leaders, more specifically, older mature men, to model and talk about true manhood and fatherhood. With fatherless guys (either physically or emotionally absent), this is paramount. The association with others who are involved in more mainstream routines of work, school, church, and family can be a beacon of normalcy for these guys. These guys need attention and affirmation. They have been getting it in all the wrong places and it is leading nowhere.

Finally, the element of a faith community, with all their spiritual experiences, can be an anchor that keeps them secure in a storm of turbulent life experiences. The percentage of disadvantaged and disenfranchised guys (and their girlfriends) has risen dramatically.

The percentage of disadvantaged and disenfranchised has risen dramatically.

They are no longer a small fringe group of kids; they are more noticeable now. Intergenerational youth ministry needs to be aggressive in connecting them with their churches and ministries. Make no apologies about your church or ministry or the fact that you desire for them to be a part of it, even if it's simply for their own good.

CONCLUSION

To bring this full circle, intergenerational youth ministry is nothing new. But for some, it has been abandoned. It needs to be revisited and it needs to be on purpose. An atmosphere of dependence on and a need for all the generations should be cultivated, with the right people doing the right things in the right places. What better place to foster community among the generations, than within a church family:

* Everyone benefits.

* Weaknesses can be strengthened by others.

* Inexperience will give way to those who have experience.

* Teachers will have students.

* Students will be taught.

* Spiritual maturity will trump immaturity.

* Mentors will mentor.

* Teenagers will be reconciled to God when, for the longest time, they have been estranged from Him.

* It makes plenty of sense.

REVIEW QUESTIONS

1. Who comes to your mind, when you think of intergenerational involvement among students?

2. Can you come up with some biblical examples of intergenerational ministry that would reinforce the importance of this kind of ministry?

3. What are some social consequences that you have observed in your own community due to the absence of intergenerational involvement?

4. Find the mean (the average), mode (the age that occurs most often), and median (the age in the middle...in order to find the median, you have to put the ages in order from lowest to highest, then find the age that is exactly in the middle) age of

those working among your students. Are there any pros and cons as well as any ministry course corrections that may need to be made?

5. What characteristics in your life would cause students to listen to or want to be like you?

CHAPTER 8

Welcome to Varsity:
Transitioning Middle-Schoolers to High School

Gretchen was sixteen when she was asked to go to camp by one of her friends at school. Gretchen had never been to anything the church sponsored but was interested in getting away from her home for a week and meeting some cute guys at camp. Camp opened up a whole new world to Gretchen. At camp she got saved and later in the week she had a heart-to-heart talk with her counselor about some of the things in her life she knew were not right. Her counselor gave her a three-step plan to have victory in those areas and she went home secure in her new relationship with God and armed with a plan to live for Him.

And she did live for God. She was radically different at home and at school. Her interests changed and she began revolving her schedule around the youth group. She was there Sunday, Wednesday, and Friday nights. Her twelve-year old brother, Kent, began to notice the change in Gretchen and when she invited him to go to youth group with her, he decided to give it a try.

The first time Kent went, it was a Wednesday night. It didn't go well at all for Kent. Gretchen told Kent he would love it. She said, "They play awesome games, they have great songs, and the Bible study is so good and everybody is so loving." But Kent didn't click with any of it. The songs were completely unfamiliar and he couldn't even sing them because his voice was changing. The game looked fun but he couldn't compete with all those older guys. The Bible study was boring and none of the students were kind and loving like Gretchen had said. Gretchen was really surprised when Kent said he didn't want to go back.

Does it have to be that way in your student ministry? Can you have a dynamic student ministry that transitions middle school students into the high school ministry with relative ease?

Well, maybe it can't be done with ease. Mark Twain wryly said, "When a boy turns 13, stick him in a barrel and feed him through the knot hole. When he turns 16 plug up the knot hole."[1] Nevertheless, the transition can be made very effectively in your student ministry.

To help you with this transition, I want to accomplish three things in this chapter:

* I want to identify the age group characteristics of middle school and high school students.

* I want to highlight the differences.

* I want to propose some ministry steps that will help you as you seek to move your students along from the middle school to the high school student ministry.

PREPARE FOR TRANSITION ARMED WITH THE KNOWLEDGE OF YOUR STUDENT'S AGE GROUP CHARACTERISTICS AND DIFFERENCES

CHARACTERISTICS OF MIDDLE SCHOOL STUDENTS	CHARACTERISTICS OF HIGH SCHOOL STUDENTS	DIFFERENCES TO KEEP IN MIND
Physical:	**Physical:**	**Physical:**
∗ Accelerated changes in physical appearance are occurring: 　◆ They become taller and heavier 　◆ Their appetites increase 　◆ Their faces and bodies become more mature ∗ Marked differences in development between genders 　◆ Boys usually begin a bit later than girls ∗ Energetic and fun ∗ Experience fatigue easily ∗ A relatively short attention span	∗ Concerned about image 　◆ May become neater and more concerned with what they wear 　◆ May seek to please a certain sub-culture with their appearance ∗ Growth spurt slows down 　◆ Some begin to fill out rather than grow up 　◆ Some begin to mature and lose their "baby fat" ∗ Have realistic view of limits to which body can be tested	∗ Keep in mind that generally middle school students cannot compete with high school students in activities and athletic competitions. ∗ When planning activities, remember that middle school students wear out a lot faster than their high school counterparts. ∗ Your high school students will not lose interest as easily as the middle school students in an activity.
Social:	**Social:**	**Social:**
∗ Look to friends for approval ∗ Attracted to the opposite sex ∗ Relationships are complicated to them ∗ Seek role models ∗ Question authority and family values ∗ Seek acceptance and trust ∗ Task-oriented and competitive ∗ Tend to reject ready-made solutions	∗ Want intimacy in relationships ∗ Want to be respected ∗ Test sexual attractiveness ∗ Want adult-like leadership roles ∗ Able to commit and follow through ∗ See adults as fallible ∗ Apt to reject goals set by others ∗ Renegotiate relationships	∗ Friendships for your high school students will be a lot closer and more meaningful than the middle school students. ∗ Your high school students will tend to be more responsive and respectful to leadership. ∗ Your middle school students will need short-term easy-to-reach goals, whereas your high school students can grasp and accomplish longer-term goals.

CHARACTERISTICS OF MIDDLE SCHOOL STUDENTS	CHARACTERISTICS OF HIGH SCHOOL STUDENTS	DIFFERENCES TO KEEP IN MIND
Emotional:	**Emotional:**	**Emotional:**
* Tend to be moody, restless, unpredictable, and argumentative * Compare themselves to others * Apprehensive about physical changes and emerging sexuality * Anxious to be accepted by their peer group * Want privacy and independence from adults * Want to be part of something important * See selves as always on center stage * Body changes and differences can cause situations of embarrassment * Easily offended * Becoming cynical and untrusting of adults including their parents * Strive for independence yet want and need parents' help.	* Want to be seen as individuals while conforming to certain peer standards * Want autonomy * Want to determine what happens in their world * Desire respect * Beginning to accept and enjoy their own uniqueness * Developing their own set of values and beliefs * Introspective * Can see self from the viewpoint of others * Can initiate and carry out tasks without supervision * Search for career possibilities * Look for confidence of others in their decisions	* Your middle school students will have a harder time with cynicism than the high school students. * Be careful not to put your middle school students in situations where they would be embarrassed but find ways to stretch your high school students. * Challenge your high school students to step up and change their world, but challenge your middle school students to do group projects that will make a difference. * Help middle school students to work through their life step-by-step but help high school students to set long-term goals.
Intellectual:	**Intellectual:**	**Intellectual:**
* Concerned with equity and justice * Beginning to think abstractly * Understand cause and effect * Can handle in-depth short-term projects * Challenge assumptions * Want to explore beyond community * Can imagine consequences * Moved from fantasy to realistic focus on life's goals.	* Mastering abstract thinking * Like demonstrating acquired knowledge * Develop theories to explain and make sense of things * Create new possibilities from information * Can consider issues from man's perspectives * Grow impatient with meaningless activity * Can imagine impact of present behavior on future	* Get your junior high students involved in discussions with "yes," "no," and "why" questions while encouraging high school students to explain their thoughts and views on issues. * Give opportunities for high school students to interact in small groups with a discussion leader from the group. Give opportunities for middle school students to learn from leadership in small group settings.

MINISTRY POINTERS
FOR MIDDLE SCHOOL STUDENTS
TO PREPARE FOR TRANSITION:

1. Make a transition with your purpose:

a. The purpose of middle school ministry is to develop in middle school students a personal awareness of what God wants to do in their lives.

* An awareness of God's plan of salvation.

2 Peter 3:9 - The Lord is not slack concerning His promise, as some count slackness, but is longsuffering toward us, not willing that any should perish but that all should come to repentance.

* An awareness of God's plan for separation from the world.

1 John 2:15-16 - Do not love the world or the things in the world. If anyone loves the world, the love of the Father is not in him. For all that is in the world—the lust of the flesh, the lust of the eyes, and the pride of life—is not of the Father but is of the world.

* An awareness of God's plan for using Scripture to combat the tricks of Satan and the temptations of the world.

2 Timothy 3:16-17 - All Scripture is given by inspiration of God, and is profitable for doctrine, for reproof, for correction, for instruction in righteousness, that the man of God may be complete, thoroughly equipped for every good work.

* An awareness of God's plan in giving us His Spirit to help us by convicting us of sin, guiding us to God's will, and encouraging us as we move through life.

John 16:8-11 - And when He has come, He will convict the world of sin, and of righteousness, and of judgment: of sin, because they do not believe in Me; of righteousness, because I go to My Father and you see Me no more; of judgment, because the ruler of this world is judged.

b. The purpose of senior high ministry is to develop in your senior high students a passionate walk with God.

As you move through the transition with your students from middle school to high school, I believe your purpose changes.

Think about it: Your students are moving from the concrete dependent world of an eleven-year old to the abstract-thinking, totally independent world of an eighteen-year old. During these years, most of the determinative decisions that will govern their life will be made:

* Where will I go to college?

* What vocation will I go into?

* Who will my life-long friends be?

* What standards will I have for a spouse?

It is crucial for them to develop a passionate walk with God.

c. How does this happen?

* Our high school students need to discover that their relationship with God is a daily walk.

Our high school students need to discover that their relationship with God is a daily walk.

Colossians 1:10 - That you may walk worthy of the Lord, fully pleasing Him, being fruitful in every good work and increasing in the knowledge of God.

Psalm 68:19 - Blessed be the Lord, Who daily loads us with benefits, the God of our salvation!

The daily grind of school, work, friends, parents, and the stuff life is made of takes a toll on our students; so they need to know that our Lord has a daily plan to help them succeed and not fail.

* We also need to teach our high school students that it is a satisfying walk.

John 10:10 - I have come that they may have life, and that they may have it more abundantly.

1 John 1:4 - And these things we write to you that your joy may be full.

I believe that many young people feel that God's work is like the game at Chuck-E-Cheese called "Whack-a-Mole." In that game, as the moles come up out of their holes you bust them in the head. Many students feel that when they do anything that is really fun, God busts on them. They need to know that God is not trying to be a spoil sport. His plan for their life is awesome.

* We need to teach our high school students that it is a dynamic walk. Most Christian high school-age students never consider that God has a dynamic plan for their life. If a student pursues this plan they can accomplish great things for God.

Jeremiah 29:11 - For I know the thoughts that I think toward you, says the LORD, thoughts of peace and not of evil, to give you a future and a hope.

* Finally, we need to teach our senior high students that their walk with God is a focused walk.

When I was eighteen, I dedicated my life to the Lord because a man preached a message at a dedication service at Word of Life Island. He said this: "If your life doesn't count for God then it doesn't count for anything." That phrase changed my life. I began to focus my life on making a difference for God. We really need to present to our high school students that God has an incredible plan for them and that there are only two things that will go to Heaven with them: the Word of God and the souls of men.

1 Peter 1:25 - But the word of the LORD endures forever."

2. Prepare for the transition with your program.

a. Make a transition in activities.

Purpose **is an operative word.** Everything you do in any student meeting should have focus and purpose. What is the ultimate purpose in every activity?

Keep these concepts in mind:

When your students are in middle school, you should focus on games that are non-athletic and fun. At this awkward age, to play traditional sports creates embarrassment and hesitancy. So you will want to devise games that create spirit and expend energy.

This week I spoke at a youth group that was having an evangelistic outreach. Mostly middle school students showed up—about forty-five of them. The leader led them in a game called *Human Pin Ball*. It was a variation of dodge ball, without teams. If you got hit with the ball you had to sit down but if you caught the ball sitting down you could hit somebody standing up and get back into the game.

Those middle school students were having a wild time.

One more thing about middle school games: don't let them get boring. When it seems like the students have peaked in excitement and are having the time of their life, cut the game off. That way, they will get excited about it next time.

On the other hand, with your senior high students you should focus on teamwork and competition. Traditional sports are fine with fun variations. By planning these types of activities, you will motivate teamwork, spirit, and energy in your youth group.

b. Make a transition with your meeting schedule.

With middle school students, almost every minute has to be scheduled or you run the risk of losing control; but with senior high students, you can have more informal fellowship times that are unstructured so that the students can "hang out" together.

Recently, I have seen many high school programs use the coffee house type atmosphere with good results. The reason this approach is effective is because it is a casual atmosphere, with a lot of opportunity for casual fellowship. It is less formal, allowing you much variation in the meeting itself.

c. Make a transition with your personal approach to students.

Discipline

* Handling middle school discipline problems should include individual, personal confrontation with clear communication about unacceptable behavior and clear boundaries to follow in the future. Clear biblical instruction should be given to identify wrong behavior and acceptable behavior.

* Senior high discipline problems should include individual, personal confrontation with an approach that allows the student to think through what he or she did wrong as well as look into the Word of God to theorize how they should have responded in the situation.

Discipleship

* Discipleship of middle school students is a little more complicated than senior high students. Middle school students wake up in a different world every day and they lose interest in long-term assignments, so you have to give clear, very defined, short-range goals to work on.

  Looking back to my middle school years, I was motivated to a more consistent daily quiet time with God when my student leader asked me to just try reading the Bible and praying for seven minutes per day.

* Discipleship of senior high students should be done personally as much as possible with the emphasis on life change. Follow the pattern in 2 Timothy 2:1-2: You therefore, my son, be strong in the grace that is in Christ Jesus. And the things that you have heard from me among many witnesses, commit these to faithful men who will

be able to teach others also. You want to identify sinful patterns in their lives and use the Word of God to devise a plan to change.

Casual connections

* Keep in mind that middle school students feel awkward in their interactions with adults. Their friends are their world, so give them opportunities to connect with groups and focus on creating credibility.

* With your senior high students you should focus on creating relationships that are built on respect. Your strategy should be to model a passionate life that they will desire. The Word of God says it this way in Philippians 2:15:That you may become blameless and harmless, children of God without fault in the midst of a crooked and perverse generation, among whom you shine as lights in the world.

Teaching

* Teaching middle school students is a challenge. Because of the fact that they view life in high definition (commercials, text messages, video games, and YouTube), they have a short attention span for Bible study. Because of this, you need to plan your teaching ministry so that your lecture segments are no more than ten to twelve minutes and are spiced up with visuals, group dynamics, and projects.

* Your senior high students on the other hand need to be able to think on their own. So even though their attention span is a little longer, you should strive to get them involved in learning the Bible together. Challenge their minds to read the Word, think about it, and apply it. Your group dynamics should be more mature and should motivate your students to work together to come up with answers.

3. Prepare for the transition with your parents.

Recently I was in a group discussion with some men from my ministry. One of the men who had a son in seventh grade said, "I am really concerned about my son. Just all of a sudden, I hear him talking to his mom with disrespect."

I don't want to condone disrespect of any kind, but wouldn't it be helpful for that dad to know that this kind of behavior is normal for a seventh grader?

As you discuss middle school characteristics with parents of middle school students, remember to discuss the following:

a. Help parents realize that adolescence is the time when students are working toward independence

Parents need to talk to their middle school students about the fact that they are accountable to God for their decisions. They will have every opportunity to sin and they need to make a decision in each situation that will please God, not necessarily the parents.

It is also important for parents to realize that every time a middle school son or daughter makes an attempt at independence, it is not a rejection of the parents but an attempt to find their boundaries and their freedom. Then, as the student transitions into high school, the parents need to remember to choose their battles wisely. Some minor issues can be ignored, but bigger issues need to be addressed from a biblical standpoint with the goal of making decisions that please God.

b. Help parents to realize that what all adolescents need is a stable family.

Throughout their adolescence, every teenager is crying out for a person with skin on to come alongside them, offering the gift of a gentle and caring presence. Remember, middle school students are looking for role models, so it is vitally important for the parents to make their Christianity work at home. As a student moves

Remember, middle school students are looking for role models.

from middle school into high school, it is vitally important to see a biblical model in the home.

c. Help your students' parents to develop the art of being a listener.

   ✳ Few parents have the patience to truly listen to a middle school student. Because of that, by the time these students are in high school, they are convinced that nobody really cares how they feel about things.

   ✳ When it comes to training and nurturing our middle school students, the parents have to remember that they hold all the cards. They may not feel like it, especially when they feel like they have been taken advantage of by their son or daughter. But the fact is they do have all the power they need to lead their middle school students.

   ✳ The parents are responsible to listen to their student.

   ✳ To really listen to their child, they have to put their agenda in the background at first. Then they must do all they can to get inside the head and the heart of the student

   ✳ Parents need to be adept at reading their children's eyes and listening for the reasons they feel the way they do.

   Recently one of my students looked at me and said, "Mr. Phillips, are you even listening to me?" Why did they feel that way? The student felt that way because I was fooling around with something on my desk while they were pouring their heart out to me. Shame on me!

   ✳ The first place to start with any issue or problem is by asking questions.

   ✳ The goal of listening to the student is to seek to create a climate of trust that will allow the truth to come out.

d. Help parents realize the most effective ways to discipline their students as they go through the transition.

   ✳ Middle school students need firm, strong, loving discipline. The boundaries need to be clear and the consequences for unacceptable behavior need to be defined.

* For high school students, boundaries and consequences can be negotiated. This allows the student to be able to be involved in their destiny and think about it from their perspective and the parent's perspective.

Can you minister to Gretchen and Kent in the same church, even though one is in middle school and one is in high school? Yes. Know your students, know your parents, and model a dynamic relationship with God yourself.

If you plan carefully, your youth ministry will be like a factory. You will take young, loud, obnoxious, middle school students and move them through the transition from middle school to high school to become vibrant, passionate, young adults that are focused on doing great things for God.

How will you measure the success of your program in ten years? One of the ways will be to evaluate how well you did transitioning them from middle school to high school.

How will you measure the success of your program in ten years?

REVIEW QUESTIONS

1. What is a biblical purpose for middle school student ministry?
2. What is a biblical purpose for high school student ministry?
3. How can you help parents with their teens' transition from middle school to high school?
4. What would the end product look like if you made this transition effectively?
5. What action plan can you take right now to make your transition more effective?

CHAPTER 9

Molding Her Heart:
Mentoring Girls

It wasn't too long ago that I was seated in a chair with a half-desk attached to the front. Like a good little ministry student, I had my notebook out and pen ready. Prepared as I was, it was the question and response that was soon to follow that I wasn't ready for. The professor took his place at the front of the room and opened our class that day by asking us to respond to a question. He lobbed and we responded. "How many of you could say that you were discipled by an older godly adult while growing up?" One or two hands found their way into the air, while the other sixty-some of us sat there looking around.

My thoughts were "Really! We are all a bunch of pastor's, missionary's, deacon's, and other *super spiritual* type person's kids and only a *few* of us have been discipled!" I quickly saw the need for the question. There we sat in a discipleship class, ready and willing to be taught how we should go about training up a generation of teenagers in the principles and truths of God. If the truth were told, none of us had a clue how to disciple or mentor anyone. The professor knew that the most important thing for us to see, right from the start of the semester, was

None of us had a clue how to disciple or mentor anyone.

the shortage of discipleship going on in the Christian churches and homes of America today.

We live in such a fast-paced society. Many of our churches have become so concerned with putting on a good, fast-paced show to keep the attention of our ADD-ridden generation that the simplicity and discipline needed to be a consistent Christ-follower somehow gets left in the dust. Why do we need to disciple or mentor our students? First and foremost, because we are commanded to do so. Matthew 28:19 says, "Go therefore and make disciples of all nations." It does not say, "Go and make converts, and then entertain them so that they will stay in church." I am not attempting to be harsh or say that good productions are unbiblical — far from it. I am simply trying to wave a yellow flag and beckon the student ministers and volunteers of today to slow down and consider the importance of effective mentorship and discipleship relationships. I am saying that perhaps the account we need to take is to look at our students ten, fifteen years from now. Are they following Christ? Are their lives models for younger generations to imitate? Bottom line for us: how can we be more effective at training up disciples of Jesus Christ?

This should not cause us to despair, but spur us on to seek out the heart of God. His Word is living and active and sharper than any two-edged sword. He divides hearts, conquers nations, and is even now asking us to listen closely. His message to us about mentorship in our ministries is vital and timely. I implore you to listen closely to what the Holy Spirit awakens in your heart over the next few pages. If we let Him, He desires to eternally change us and those we influence, molding all of us into the image of His Son (Romans 8:29).

WHAT IS MENTORSHIP?

There are many definitions of mentorship. Most would agree that mentorship entails an older professional who downloads all of their knowledge to a younger student who is seeking proficiency in her mentor's profession. While I fully agree with that summation, I would like to submit a new twist on this typical definition of mentorship. I would say that true biblical mentorship would be defined like this: *an older woman of discretion, integrity, discipline, and holiness, who is willing to be broken bread and poured-out wine so that a younger woman can be fully trained in the reality and truth of following the Lord the way He longs to be followed.*

You see, it is one thing to agree to share your knowledge about how to bake a cake or run a company. That form of mentorship is the one that the world celebrates and holds in high esteem — one person downloading knowledge into another. While this is an important part of mentorship, it is only a *part*. We saw Jesus download lots and lots of information into his disciples, but more importantly we saw Him living a pattern of obedience, teachability, and integrity. Society exploits a "do as I say, not as I do" mantra. Jesus never promoted such nonsense. He never asked His disciples to do anything He did not first model for them. Titus 2 lays out for us not only a clear command for older women to mentor younger women, but also spells out what characteristics are to define the older women so that they will be effective mentors. Titus 2:3-4a says to teach "the older women likewise, that they be reverent in behavior, not slanderers, not given to

It is important to soak in this truth — that the call to mentor comes with a cost.

much wine, teachers of good things— that they admonish the young women." There is a reason that the qualifications for the mentor are listed first. It is important to soak in this truth — that the call to mentor comes with a cost.

I love the first part of verse 3 in Titus 2. It says, "That they be reverent in behavior." *Revere* is the root word of reverent. To revere someone is *to hold them in high esteem and to regard them with deep respect.* To be reverent toward something is much the same: it is to hold deep feelings of respect. In other words, as godly women called to mentor, our behavior is to exude high esteem and respect for our Heavenly Father. All things that we do or involve ourselves in are to lift high and make much of our Redeemer, our Savoir, Jesus Christ. This is so vital for us to fully grasp! If our actions begin to be clearly motivated by a deep-seated adoration, respect, and love for our Savior, several really amazing things happen. Number one, we stop living our lives by "do" and "don't do" checklists. We remember that although 1 Corinthians 10:23 (NIV) begins with "everything is permissible" it then continues with "but not everything is beneficial." Sure, we have tons of freedom in Christ, but we have a responsibility and a calling to make sure our behavior and our actions reflect a reverence to our Savior and King. How would our girls begin to respond if we dared to live lives defined by reverence instead of rules? I believe the result would be epic.

Secondly, as we live reverent lives we experience the *best* that Jesus is constantly beckoning us toward. In John 10:10 Jesus told His listeners that while a thief comes to steal, kill, and destroy He has come that they may have a more abundant life. We completely miss out on abundant lives when our focus is a list of rules or when we are bound and determined to use all the liberties our "freedom in Christ" offers us. Life-reflecting reverence and awe over the redemption we have been freely given allows our eyes to be stayed upon our Savior and Redeemer, our hearts to be sensitive to His instruction, and our lives to experience true abundance. Lastly, reverent behavior allows us to speak boldly the words Paul declared: "Imitate me, just as I also imitate Christ" (1 Corinthians 11:1) It gives us the freedom and confidence to let our lives say, "It's OK. Do what I am doing. It honors God; it makes much of our Savoir and it is abundant!" We are to be women who deeply respect our Savior and King.

We are to be women who deeply respect our Savior and King.

There is another little phrase following "that they be reverent in behavior" in Titus 2:3 that may step on our toes: "not slanderers." To slander is defined as *the act of saying something false or malicious that damages someone's reputation.* Slander can take on a few different forms. As women, it is so easy for us to be guilty of slander. We talk about each other, claw to get to the top, and smile piously at someone who is cuter than we are. I know that we serve a God Who knows all things and is wise beyond measure. One of the many reasons I am convinced of this is because He knew to specifically call us out on slander so that we could be effective mentors. How can we possibly walk around gossiping, sharing things we know we shouldn't, snubbing other women, and honestly look into a student's eyes and say, "follow me as I follow Christ"? To think that we could or should is absurd. Girls will not be attracted to model your life if you exude the same eighth-grade, gossipy characteristics as their friends. They won't trust your instruction or insight any more than they trust the girls their own age. Our responsibility as older women is to exhort, build up, and encourage, not only one another, but also our Savior. We bear His name — we are *Christ*ians. So, when we behave poorly, or when we spend our time gossiping, spreading rumors, or joking crudely, we are putting our Savior's reputation on the line.

Slander isn't just applicable on a parallel level (us and other people); it is equally as dangerous vertically (us and God the Father). We are to live lives that are gracious in speech, holding others in high esteem as redeemed, worthy, and anointed daughters of the Most High God. If the Creator of the universe places that kind of value on us, shouldn't we place that kind of value on each other? Our heart's prayer should be that of David's in Psalm 19:14: "Let the words of my mouth and the meditation of my heart be acceptable in Your sight, O LORD, my strength and my Redeemer."

Completing the triplet of things we *are not* to do as godly older women, Paul says, "not given to much wine." Simply put, offering control of your body over to *anything* other than Christ is unwise behavior. Our students live in a culture where drinking

> **Simply put, offering control of your body over to anything other than Christ is unwise behavior.**

is acceptable and even expected in order to run in the popular crowd. As older women our behavior is not to reflect that of an irresponsible teenager who is defining their life by culture and being reckless with their actions and body. As mentors, leaders, and followers of Christ, our lives are to be filled with the Spirit of Christ. I like the way Paul went into some detail with the church at Ephesus in Ephesians 5:15-18, saying, "See then that you walk circumspectly, not as fools but as wise, redeeming the time, because the days are evil. Therefore do not be unwise, but understand what the will of the Lord is. And do not be drunk with wine, in which is dissipation; but be filled with the Spirit." We are to be women who understand that time is short. We cannot be found wasting our time with alcohol, or filling ourselves with anything that desensitizes us to what the Holy Spirit is trying to speak into our lives. A generation of young women is watching our every move and we are not promised tomorrow. As women who are called to mentor, this realization should greatly affect who we are and what we do.

Verse 3 ends by listing one thing we are to do as mentors: we are to be teachers of good things. Lucky for us, Paul goes on to list the "good things" we are to be teaching! Titus 2:4-5: "Admonish the young women to love their husbands, to love their children, to be discreet, chaste, homemakers, good, obedient to their own husbands, that the word of God may not be blasphemed." This is by no means an exhaustive list of things we are to teach younger women, but it does list key things that only godly, older women would be qualified to teach.

THE NEED FOR MENTORSHIP

In a society where truth is defined by billboards, TV psychology, and pop culture, it is extremely difficult for a young woman to grow up with a correct view of herself and her surroundings, much less any clear view on her life purpose. To date, our answer as a society has been for a few women to rise up and begin rallies where young women gather in hordes to watch modesty fashion shows and hear talks on saving sex for marriage. Please don't misunderstand me; these are great things. They are even needed things. But they should not be the end of our attempt at redirecting a hungry generation of young women toward the truth of who they are in Christ Jesus. Our girls need to hear and know deeply that their value and worth was placed on them at creation and in them at salvation.

Our girls need to hear and know deeply that their value and worth was placed on them at creation and in them at salvation.

They did not do anything to earn it and therefore they cannot do anything to lose it. The truth is that the very Son of the living God now takes up residence within them and that when God the Father looks down at them He does not see their flaws and their sin, He sees His Son. He looks at them and sees holiness, He sees righteousness, He sees redemption, He sees what they were created to be. He also sees what needs to happen in their lives for them to realize and truly live in the abundance for which He created them and died to grant access.

My heart is so burdened for a generation of godly women to be raised up, to answer the call in Titus 2 that commands older women to train up younger women in truth. The reality is that if we continue to address symptoms with our young women, we will continue to get what we have gotten in the past: lots and lots of work, with very few dividends to show for it. If we truly desire to effect real, authentic change in the lives of the up-and-coming generation of young women, we must go deeper with them. The girls need to know why they are supposed to dress modestly, and why they should strive for purity. At some point, we have to stop placating society and saying they should do these things so that they don't get raped because their clothes are sending the wrong message, or they should avoid sex because of the high risk of sexually transmitted diseases or pregnancy. While these things may be valid and true in their own right, they are not the real reason we choose modesty or abstinence. We choose these things because there is a Creator God Who, in the very face of our evident disdain and disinterest, declared that He loved us regardless of whether we loved Him back. He sent His one and only Son to bring healing and hope to a lost and lonely world. Mentorship is so important, because it gives us the opportunity to take away the check lists of "do's and don'ts" and replace it with awestruck reverence and respect toward God's display of matchless love and holiness. I truly believe that if our girls begin to grasp this, if they begin to be changed from the inside out, we will see a revolution of unprecedented proportions in our time. Let's train up a generation of girls who dare to be different because Jesus changed their lives and because His holiness demands it.

I am excited to be one of the few women who have the opportunity to work full-time in a student ministry as the Girl's Director. I pray that more and more churches will be awakened to the desperate need our female students have to be trained up by godly older women. Student pastors are so very vital, but often they are male, and let's just be honest, it is hard for a guy to train up a young woman in becoming the godly woman she is supposed to be! However, I understand that 1) many student ministries cannot financially support a full-time Girl's Director; and 2) even the ones that can afford it would find it impossible to effectively disciple or mentor fifty, two hundred, or eight hundred girls. It is not only ridiculous, but pompous to think that this would be a possibility. It is in response to this realization that the Lord has taken me to Ephesians 4. It was after reading this chapter that I became convicted to base my ministry to female students around their discipleship. Here is why: in verse 7, Paul says that each of us have been apportioned grace, and in verse 11, he says that each of us have been given spiritual gifts.

The spiritual gifts given us serve a purpose — a grand purpose, actually. Verses 12-13 say we are given gifts "for the equipping of the saints for the work of ministry, for the edifying of the body of Christ, till we all come to the unity of the faith and of the knowledge of the Son of God, to a perfect man, to the measure of the stature of the fullness of Christ." This is so vitally important because Romans 8:29 says we have been predestined to be conformed into the image of the Son of God. Our *destiny* is to be made like the holy God. Therefore, all of our circumstances, our experiences — good and bad — serve one purpose: to conform us into the likeness of the Son of God. Why would mentoring be any different? Our highest purpose as mentors is to equip and train up a generation "to the measure of the stature of the fullness of Christ."

> **Our highest purpose as mentors is to equip and train up a generation "to the measure of the stature of the fullness of Christ."**

This is extremely important because in verse 14 of Ephesians 4, it says that if we are faithful to use our gifts, the next generation will "no longer be children, tossed to and fro and carried about with every wind of doctrine, by the trickery of men, in the cunning craftiness of deceitful plotting." It goes on to say that instead of this, the next generation, along with us, will instead speak "the truth in love" and "grow up in all things into Him who is the head—Christ".

I about jumped right out of my skin when I read this passage. I am sure that the next day at church I shared it with any and everyone who would listen to me. I had been asking the Lord how I should run an effective girls ministry, and He answered loud and clear: *"Discipleship, mentorship!* Train up the next generation of young women to live lives that reflect Me. Teach them about Me. Through this I will conform each girl and you into the likeness of My Son, so that together you can speak out My truth, standing firm and causing a lost world to stand in awe of *Me."*

That's it. That is what it is all about. True ministry to girls is about godly women stepping up to the plate and teaching truth that causes a carnal, lost, dying world to stand in awe of God.

THE CONTENT OF MENTORSHIP

So I am praying that each of you, as you have read and listened with your heart, have heard the beckoning of our Holy God to step up and mentor the young women within our circle of influence. If you are anything like me and you have heard this call, your next question will be *"How!?"* If that is the case, then I am glad you asked. As we wrap up our time together, I want to share with you a few practical steps toward implementing mentorship, both in your personal life as well as your ministry.

First, it is important to take part in mentorship personally. If you do not already have one, I would highly encourage you to seek the Lord as to whom you should ask to mentor *you*. Ministry can absolutely drain you dry if you let it. For me, I sought the Lord for almost a year before the Lord blessed me with a mentor. However, it was time well spent — she is amazing!

Second, I would encourage you to seek the Lord as to who He would have you mentor personally. It can be difficult to know who you should mentor. This is why you must be fervent in prayer as you wait for the Lord to direct you to that one or those couple students you are to pour your life into. When the Lord gives you clear direction, go in boldness. Do not allow the attack of the enemy to cause you to back down when pushy parents ask why you aren't mentoring *their* student.

It is important when mentoring students, to be sure there is structure as to when you meet, where you meet, and what you discuss while you meet. Structure is important because: it helps the parents know how to schedule their student's activities; it allows for consistency in the student's life (which some students have very little of!); and it demands that each meeting be intentional. This structure should be pretty firmly adhered to for middle school students. High school students on the other hand can be a little more flexible and may enjoy a change every once in a while; for instance changing location of your meeting spot every couple of months or so.

Since we live in a coffee shop-driven society, those are always great places to find a quiet corner and meet with your mentor. Other good spots would be: a public park, ice cream store, or at your home. (Please use wisdom with this!) Once you arrive at your designated spot, have a plan as to what you will talk through or study. It is a good idea to start with the basics. The point of mentorship at its heart, is to reproduce Christ-followers who are equipped to stand alone and train up the generation after them. Therefore, the first six months to a year of your meeting together should heavily consist of you teaching them how to study their Bible (i.e. using Bible study methods like topical or inductive), how to have an effective prayer life, and how to cultivate spiritual disciplines like fasting, simplicity, Scripture memorization and journaling. Once you feel your mentee has a good grasp on these vital concepts, you need to encourage them to begin pouring out. Teach them to mentor girls younger than them. They can begin getting into this habit by assisting in a children's Sunday school class, or (for high school girls) attending a middle school camp as a co-leader. It is *never* too early to teach our girls to pour back out what has been poured into them. We don't want any moldy sponges! So help them be squeezed!

As a student leader, the need for mentorship among your girls will far surpass your personal ability. This can be a tough realization, but should not be discouraging at all! This need demands that the church act as the body of Christ. This need allows women from all walks of life to step into the student ministry and serve as discipleship leaders and mentors. I have had the opportunity to implement something like this within my ministry and it has been amazing! For about five or six months, I sought the Lord and spoke in different ministries at my church. I shared with them Ephesians 4 and asked them to pray and consider coming and helping mentor or disciple our female students. As one student leader to another, I interviewed *a lot* of people, but only brought on a few. The result was an amazing group of godly women ready and willing to take hungry girls deep into the truth of God.

I am sharing this with you to encourage you not to settle. As you seek the Lord for ladies to mentor alongside of you, be patient and wait for the best God desires to send. The *best* is not defined by personality, position, financial status, or ethnicity. The best is defined by godly women who meet the qualifications of Titus 2 and have a passion to pour their lives into female students. It is my experience that if you wait for this caliber of woman, you will see evident change in your girls very soon after they begin mentoring. I have also found that running twelve-week programs is a great way to offer structure and consistency, while avoiding burn out—both for your students and for your leaders. At minimum, there should be two semesters of twelve-week programs, one in the spring and one in the fall. Ideally, you would be able to run one during the summer as well. For my girls and this ministry, the summer is so busy that while the mentors and mentees still meet occasionally over the summer, it is not as highly structured as it is in the spring and the fall.

As a part of the structure, the girls sign commitment sheets at the beginning of each semester. Their leader signs it too, each of them committing to take their time together seriously and to attend each weekly meeting, to the best of their ability. This helps your leaders and your students know how serious and important mentorship is. If you treat it seriously, they will take it seriously. In addition, each week the girls fill out accountability sheets to turn into their mentor. These sheets ask questions like: "Were you consistently in God's Word this week?" and "What specific things are you struggling with right now?" There are monthly accountability sheets for the leaders. This helps me as the Girl's Director to make sure that each of my ladies is maintaining an intimate walk with the Lord, is spending enough time with her family, and isn't becoming burnt-out, or feeling overwhelmed. On those monthly sheets I also ask the leaders to tell me what the Lord is doing in the lives of their girls. This helps me keep a better gauge on the overall spiritual temperature of the girls in my ministry. Lastly, I also hold monthly meetings with the leaders. This gives them a chance to exchange ideas with one another, for us to talk about victories and struggles, and an opportunity for us to pray together as a team.

WRAPPING UP

Discipleship or mentoring is a vital practice that we as the body of Christ simply cannot continue to brush off or push to the wayside. If we truly desire to see authentic change in the generations of tomorrow, we must step up as mentors and take responsibility for our girls by pouring our hearts and lives into them. I pray that you are encouraged and have been awakened to the desperate need for mentorship both in our churches and homes. I know that mentorship is costly. It is time-intensive and keeps us at a high level of accountability and spiritual awareness. For these reasons, the temptation to shrink back from the high calling to mentor can come on strong, but we are not the kind of people who shrink back and are destroyed (Hebrews 10:39-40)! So, let's step up and press on, allowing the Lord to use us as vessels who effect authentic change in the leaders and world-changers of tomorrow.

> *If we truly desire to see authentic change in the generations of tomorrow, we must step up as mentors.*

REVIEW QUESTIONS

1. Were you mentored as a young adult? How did this positively or negatively affect you now?

2. Having taken a deeper look into Titus 2 and come to a fuller understanding of what a godly mentor should look like, do you consider yourself at a place to take on the responsibility of mentorship? If not, what is your plan to address this?

3. As a woman who desires to be a mentor, what is your personal growth plan (i.e. what books are you currently reading, what spiritual disciplines have become part of your daily life, etc.)?

4. Use the space below to write down some potential people you could ask to mentor you. Pray through each one. Be still before the Lord and ask Him to speak deeply to your heart.

5. Now ask the Lord to give you the names of a few potential girls that He would have you mentor. Ask Him to be clear as He shows you the one or two girls you are to pour your life into.

6. If you had the opportunity to begin mentoring a student tomorrow, what would the next twelve weeks of your time together look like (i.e. what would you study, what would your topics of conversation look like, etc.)?

CHAPTER 10

Does Evangelism Even Work Anymore?
Training Students in Outreach

Evangelism: The dying art of sharing the Gospel message verbally with friends, family, classmates, teammates, co-workers or strangers.

Do you ever get the feeling that evangelism doesn't work anymore?

Do you ever get the feeling that evangelism doesn't work anymore?

That sharing the Gospel is a dying art? That the proclamation of the message of Jesus verbally is an irrelevant throwback to a day when things were simpler and students weren't, well, so postmodern?

If you listen to some of the "experts" in youth ministry today you'll get the distinct impression that evangelism is dead. You'll hear them talking about an incarnational approach of social justice initiatives that embodies the Gospel in a way that postmodern students will embrace. In other words, you'll receive a "get-out-of-jail-free" card for actually having to share your faith, let alone train the students in your youth group to do the same.

Now I'm all for "incarnating" the message the best that we can in the power of the Holy Spirit. And I definitely believe that we should feed the poor, help the helpless, and love the unlovable. That is part of our calling as followers of Jesus.

But before Jesus ascended into Heaven He gave His followers this stark reminder: "But you shall receive power when the Holy Spirit has come upon you; and you shall be witnesses to Me in Jerusalem, and in all Judea and Samaria, and to the end of the earth" (Acts 1:8).

What you see unfold in the Book of Acts is the Gospel being taken from Jerusalem to the ends of the earth (the Roman Empire) over the course of twenty-eight chapters covering about twenty-eight years. The Book of Acts is a testament to what Jesus meant when He commanded us to go into all the world and make disciples of all nations.

The Book of Acts is a primer on how we are to continue to do ministry. We start where we are at (our "Jerusalem") and expand outwardly with the mission and message of Jesus. Just like the disciples, we are to be intentional, bold, loving, strategic, and relentless. To be anything less is to dishonor the commandment of Christ.

From my interaction with thousands of youth leaders across the country, I'm convinced that the typical youth leader in the average youth ministry is dishonoring that command. I don't think these youth leaders mean to. Most of them love Jesus, their students, and their jobs. But most are too busy managing meetings, counseling students, and solving problems to give more than lip service to evangelism.

My hope and prayer is that this chapter will challenge, encourage, and equip you to effectively mobilize your teenagers for ongoing and effective evangelism. In the process of sharing my vision for effective student evangelism, be warned that I may step on a few toes. But that happens when you come to the dance called evangelism.

To effectively prepare and equip your students to share the message of the Gospel, here are the action steps that you must take:

1. Dispel the biggest evangelism myth of all.

2. Choose to make evangelism a *real* priority.

3. Train your students to share the Gospel clearly and confidently.

Let's bust these down and drill a little deeper into each.

1. Dispel the biggest evangelism myth of all.

There are a lot of myths out there when it comes to evangelism. I believe that behind most of them is the enemy of our souls. Satan is doing everything he can to convince everyone he can that the Gospel is irrelevant to students today. Second Corinthians 4:3-4 remind us: "But even if our gospel is veiled, it is veiled to those who are perishing, whose minds the god of this age has blinded, who do not believe, lest the light of the gospel of the glory of Christ, who is the image of God, should shine on them."

There are a lot of myths out there when it comes to evangelism.

Satan blinds the eyes of unbelievers to the glorious message of Christ. I'm convinced that he is blinding the eyes of countless youth leaders as well. *To what?* To the power of the Gospel message to transform young lives!

Here is the biggest myth that he has perpetrated upon the body of Christ in recent years:

The Big Myth: "Evangelism doesn't work anymore."

Now while very few are brave enough to actually say these words, this mantra is being chanted in the form of inferences almost everywhere in youth ministry. The idea being sold is that postmodern teens are too sophisticated, too spiritually eclectic, and too mentally astute to be impacted by the dusty message of a rogue rabbi who lived two thousand years ago.

But God's Word does not lie. The Apostle Paul reminds us in Romans 1:16: "For I am not ashamed of the gospel of Christ, for it is the power of God to salvation for everyone who believes, for the Jew first and also for the Greek."

Notice a few things about this passage. First, it's the Gospel message that is the power of God for the salvation of everyone who believes. It's not me or you or our faith communities or whether or not we "incarnate" the message. (Although hopefully we do!) No, it's the message that transforms the soul of the sinner.

I don't know how a handful of propositions and a simple story can blast a soul out of the kingdom of darkness into the kingdom of light. I don't need to know. All I do know is that it does. God has chosen the proclamation of the Gospel message as the way to redeem His children from the realm of darkness. Paul asserts in Romans 10:14: "How then shall they call on Him in whom they have not believed? And how shall they believe in Him of whom they have not heard? And how shall they hear without a preacher?"

To me this whole process borders on mysticism. How can the proclamation of a simple set of propositions save a soul? How can the heart reception of a story regenerate a sinner?

I have no idea. All I know is this: God says it does. That's good enough for me.

Paul tips his hand and shows us his strategy for outreach in Romans 1:16 when he writes, "For the Jew first and also for the Greek." In Acts 17, he went to the Jews and preached the Gospel in the synagogue. The Jews in the synagogue accepted much of the Old Testament as Scripture and so I'm sure that Paul used it. Whenever Paul preached to Jews, he sprinkled his messages with healthy doses of Old Testament passages.

But later in Acts 17, when Paul is sharing the Good News with the Greeks, he has a totally different tactic. Instead of quoting the Old Testament, he shares the Gospel story from the beginning of the human race to the resurrection of Jesus. He quotes a pagan poet and makes reference to their very religious culture. Paul preached the same message to two totally different audiences.

In the same way, we must customize the way we present the Gospel to students in our culture. The students of a generation or two ago were much more like the Jews in the synagogue at the beginning of Acts 17.

Many, if not most, accepted the Word of God as the sole authority for spiritual truth; open the Bible and share, and most students would listen.

Today most students are more like the Greeks on Mar's Hill. They entertain many belief systems and merge and purge their own self-styled view of God, Jesus, and salvation. While many respect the Bible as a good book, most don't consider it the sole authority for spiritual truth.

We, like Paul, must share the same Gospel message but in a different way with these students. We must share the whole story of the Gospel. We must communicate it in a relevant way that connects with their worldview. It's not that we don't quote Scripture to them. (We do and we should!) It's that as we do, we don't assume that they accept it as the Word of God.

But the bottom line remains the same. The Gospel still works. *Yes,* we need to update our methodology. *Yes,* we need to communicate

We need to update our methodology.

the message in a relevant way. Because it is the power of God for the salvation of everyone who believes!

2. Choose to make evangelism a *real* priority.

Is evangelism a real priority in your ministry? Before you answer that, consider this: evangelism is the most over-hyped, under-done subject in ministry. Most evangelical churches in America have evangelism as part of their mission statement, purposes, or

A little advice for parents of students: 1) Every day, do something in your children's world. Every week I help my grade school daughter with her homework. Do I do it because I love it? No, at the end of the day I would rather do something else than more schoolwork. But I do it because it is important to Hannah. And because helping with homework is what a parent (I did not say a mom!) should do. 2) Discover what your children love to do, and regularly do it with them. That shows them they matter to you. Take your daughter roller skating. Shoot hoops with your son. It is really okay that you are pitiful at basketball! Just spend time with him because he loves it.

core values. Look on the average church's website and you'll find evangelism mentioned in one way or another. From slogans like, "To know Him and make Him known" to purpose statements such as, "Equipping the body of Christ here at _____ to worship God, follow Jesus, and win their world," evangelism is central to the mission statements of countless churches and student ministries.

But it's easy to put words on a flyer or website. My question is this: Is it a *real* priority?

Many youth group leaders salve their souls with thoughts like, "Well I teach my students to preach the Gospel and use words if necessary." However, God's Word makes it clear again and again that words are necessary.

Other youth leaders hide behind an annual missions trip or quarterly outreach meeting. They point to these outreach experiences as proof that evangelism is indeed a priority in their youth groups.

But evangelism is not a priority until it is done relentlessly and consistently. If I try telling my wife, "Honey, I love you, and so once a year I'm going to go on a vacation with you for a whole week and once every three months I'm going to spend an hour with you," how do you think I'll be received? Yet we do the same thing when we try to get the evangelism monkey off our backs by doing an annual missions trip and quarterly outreach meeting. Again, evangelism is not a true priority in our youth groups until we do it relentlessly and consistently.

> **But evangelism is not a priority until it is done relentlessly and consistently.**

Think about it. We say that worship is a priority and give it twenty minutes every week in our youth group meeting. We commit thirty minutes or so to the teaching of God's Word because it is a priority. In addition, we schedule fellowship and connection time because they too are priorities. But where does evangelism fit into your weekly youth group rundown?

D.L. Moody stated once, "I can tell more about a man's spiritual priorities by his checkbook than his prayer book." By the same token, I can tell more about a youth leader's priorities by his weekly program rundown sheet than his youth group's website or ministry brochure. If evangelism isn't somewhere on the list, then it is not a priority. Or, at the very minimum, it is a low priority.

So how can you make evangelism more of a priority in your youth group? Let me give you two quick ways:

a. Motivate your teens to bring their unreached friends to youth group.

Did you know that according to George Barna in *Third Millennium Teens,* nine out of ten unreached teenagers say they would come out to youth group if they were invited by their Christian friends?[1] Think about that for a moment. We are sitting on one of the greatest outreach tools in America: our weekly youth group meetings!

If your students are willing to invite their friends and most of their friends are willing to attend, then you have a tremendous opportunity to reach them for Jesus. There's something about the gathering of Christians and proclamation of the truth that is convicting for the unreached and a powerful evangelistic opportunity. Check out the words of Paul in 1 Corinthians 14:23-25: "Therefore if the whole church comes together in one place, and all speak with tongues, and there come in those who are uninformed or unbelievers, will they not say that you are out of your mind? But if all prophesy, and an unbeliever or an uninformed person comes in, he is convinced by all, he is convicted by all. And thus the secrets of his heart are revealed; and so, falling down on his face, he will worship God and report that God is truly among you."

Prophecy (or in other words, "the proclamation of God's Word") convicts and convinces an unbeliever of his sinfulness, reveals "the secrets of his heart," and causes him to fall down and repent in a powerful way. As Hebrews 4:12-13 reminds us: "For the word of God is living and powerful, and sharper than any two-edged sword, piercing even to the division of soul and spirit, and of joints and marrow, and is a discerner of the thoughts and intents of the heart. And there is no creature hidden from His sight, but all things are naked and open to the eyes of Him to whom we must give account."

What better place to have the Word of God pierce, slice, and convict than your weekly youth group meeting? When you motivate your students to bring their friends out and you teach God's Word in an accurate and relevant way, the likelihood of reaching these young people for Christ goes way, way up.

b. Present the Gospel every week.

I was raised in a youth ministry where the Gospel was presented every week at the end of each talk. And, virtually every week, students came to Jesus. Why? Because the youth leader had pounded into our heads that he was going to give the Gospel every week and that we needed to bring our unreached friends. We did and, once our friends came to Jesus, they'd bring out even more of their friends.

So when I co-started Grace Church with my good friend Rick Long eighteen years ago, we started with the same commitment. As the preaching pastor, I gave the Gospel every week and challenged the adults to bring their friends. They complied. We started with twenty-three people in a buddy's living room and when I resigned to pursue Dare 2 Share Ministries full-time, we had over one thousand people. Today Grace Church (under Rick's leadership) has exploded to 2,500 people. The most exciting thing though is not the number of people, but percentage of converts—sixty-five percent of our congregation came to Christ through our church's outreach efforts!

Is it because of our building? No! Our building is small, ugly, and old.

Is it because of our budget? No! Our budget is small, ugly, and did I mention small?

Is it because of our marketing strategy? *Yes!* And here it is: get everybody to invite their friends and give the Gospel every week.

Just as this strategy works with a group of adults at a church, it especially works with students in a youth group because students love to hang out with their friends!

While I don't have the space in the context of this chapter to bust down all of the 'whats' and 'hows' of what this looks like, I can refer you to Dare 2 Share's website which is packed full of helpful tools to equip you and your students. Go to www.dare2share.org/gowide to get started and watch your youth ministry grow with new converts.

c. Getting Personal

Allow me to disrupt your personal world for a minute here. When's the last time you shared your faith? If you are not consistently and relentlessly sharing Jesus, how can you expect your students to? After all, your title is something like "youth leader," right? You are a leader of youth. What you

When's the last time you shared your faith?

are is what you're leading them to become. If you are not a witness for Jesus then, chances are, they won't be either.

Jesus calls us all to share our faith. We may do it in different ways and with different styles but all of us are called to share the message of Jesus. After all, it's called "The Great Commission," not "The Good Suggestion."

My wife brings the Gospel up differently than I do. You probably bring it up differently than me. That's perfectly fine. As a matter of fact, it's very good. We all need to learn how to share our faith with style - our style. Paul was more of a talker. Peter was more of a stalker. Barnabas was more of a buddy. And Luke was more of a brain. They were four different followers of Jesus with four unique styles of evangelism. If it's true of the early disciples, it's true of you and me as well.

Find your style and go for it. You may stumble and fumble

and that's okay. Your students will appreciate the effort and follow your lead.

3. Train your students to share the Gospel clearly and confidently.

While motivating your teens to invite their friends to youth group and modeling sharing your faith are powerful vehicles for evangelism, your teens also need to be equipped to personally share their faith.

* Help them share it *clearly*.

Do your students know how to share the Gospel clearly? The other day I asked my twitchy six-year-old to concentrate on his homework. He was still moving around quite a bit, so finally, out of exasperation, I exclaimed, *"Jeremy, you need to settle down and concentrate, concentrate, concentrate!!!"* He looked at me in utter frustration and said, "I'm trying to Daddy, but I don't know what *concentrate* means!"

When we equip our students to share the good news of Jesus with their friends we must teach them to use language that makes sense to non-Christians. Phrases like:

"Let Jesus into your heart", "Repent of all your sins" and "Make Jesus Lord of your life" make no more sense to non-Christians than the word 'CONCENTRATE' made to my six year old. Paul prayed in Colossians 4:4 for this kind of clarity as he shared the good news of Jesus. If the great apostle Paul prayed for clarity in his Gospel presentation then how much more we need to pray for it and cultivate it.

The average student today doesn't have a context for understanding the Gospel.

The average student today doesn't have a context for understanding the Gospel.

We can provide that context by explaining what some have called "the meta-narrative" -- in other words "the big picture story" of the Gospel message.

At Dare 2 Share we equip teenagers to share this story in six scenes that play out from the first chapter of Scripture to the very last verse of Revelation. We call it The **GOSPEL** Journey:

God created us to be with Him.

GENESIS 1, 2

Our sins separate us from God.

GENESIS 3

Sins cannot be removed by good deeds.

GENESIS 4 - MALACHI 4

Paying the price for sins, Jesus died and rose again.

MATTHEW - LUKE

Everyone who trusts in Him alone has eternal life.

JOHN - JUDE

Life that's eternal means we will be with Jesus forever.

REVELATION

These are more talking points than script, and are designed to help students navigate the entire story as they share Jesus. Why not have your students know, understand, and memorize each of these points and then practice communicating these bullet points in a natural way with each other? Without training, most students don't know how to explain the Gospel in a conversational way.

It's at this point I sometimes get a little pushback from youth leaders who say, "Well, I don't want to just give my kids some method of sharing the Gospel. I want them to do it naturally. After all, teens today aren't into rote memory."

Allow me to push back for a bit. First of all, this is not so much a "method" but the "message" of the Gospel in bullet form. Secondly, if you don't help students with a simple, cogent way of sharing the message, they probably won't. Can you imagine being a coach of a basketball team who didn't have any plays for your team? That's what we do when we send our students out to evangelize without a "play" to execute. Finally, students today memorize more than ever. They memorize everything from theorems in math class to "moves" on video games to entire playbooks in sports. Why not equip them to memorize the basics of the most important message on Planet Earth?

Not long ago we filmed a quasi-reality series called *The GOSPEL Journey* where I took a Wiccan, atheist, agnostic, preacher's kid, Episcopalian, Presbyterian, and city girl to the Rocky Mountains for a six-day adventure. I basically spent one day on each of these six points of the GOSPEL and let them debate, ask questions, argue, and interact. The results were powerful!

Why? Because of me? *No!* Because the power of the Gospel is alive and well!

To check out a short video about this reality series go to www.dare2share.org/gospeljourney. I think you'll like it.

The GOSPEL Journey acrostic will help your students share the simple message of Jesus in a clear, biblically accurate way.

* Help them share it *confidently*.

In addition to knowing how to share the Gospel message clearly, your students also need to learn how to engage their unreached friends confidently and naturally in conversations about spiritual things.

During my thirty years of faith-sharing with thousands of others, I have discovered a timeless principle that I believe can help your students become more confident and effective when sharing their faith. It can be summarized by this simple equation:

$$\text{Loving}^3 \times \text{Listening}^3 \times \text{Learning}^3 = \text{Reaching}^3$$

When you love someone, listen to them, and learn from them and from God's Word, all in the power of the third person of the Trinity, something amazing happens.

Let me explain. Loving to the third power means we love others like Jesus did. As 1 Corinthians 13 tells us so eloquently, without love we gain nothing, we do nothing, we are nothing. Love should be our defining characteristic as Christians, particularly when we are sharing the message of God's gift of salvation!

Listening to the third power helps provide us with the insights we need to customize our conversations in order to meet people where they are. Part of effective listening is asking thought-provoking questions that naturally move the conversation toward God-talk. For example, questions like:

* What's most important to you in life?

* That's an awesome song. Does that one line ever make you think about God when you hear it?

* I know you're hurt by what your friend said. Do you ever take your hurt feelings to God and ask Him how you should respond?

* Why do you think there's so much suffering in the world?

Jesus was highly effective at asking people penetrating questions and listening to their responses. Check out Matthew 16:15, Mark 10:18, and Luke 20:41-44 for examples.

Learning to the third power gives us the opportunity to learn more about the other person's beliefs and about what the Bible says. When we listen and learn from others, they will be much more willing to listen and learn from us, triggering open, interactive dialogue. And when we dig into the Bible, seeking answers when difficult questions arise, the transforming truth of God's Word is unleashed.

It's essential to remember that the most important part of the L^3 equation is the third power—the Holy Spirit Himself! As we trust in Him, He will give us the ability to love, listen, and learn in His strength and not our own. He will guide our words and actions allowing us to confidently share the invaluable message of the Gospel.

A FINAL CHALLENGE

Helping your students reach out effectively is not as difficult as you might think. It's not about you or your youth group model or style of ministry. It's about the Gospel message doing its work. All you must do is unleash it and unleash your teenagers to unleash it. The Gospel message and the Holy Spirit will do the rest.

REVIEW QUESTIONS

1. Do you truly believe that evangelism works in today's culture? Why or why not?

2. If your ministry was evaluated by your program rundown sheet, would evangelism show up as a high priority? Why or why not?

3. What are specific ways you can make evangelism a higher priority?

4. How would your youth group respond if you presented the Gospel every week?

5. When was the last time you shared your faith? What happened?

6. Which part of your equation is the weakest (i.e. loving, listening, learning)?

7. What is one specific take-away from this chapter that you will put into practice immediately?

CHAPTER 11

Students on Mission:
Reaching Schools with the Gospel

"Do you remember when you challenged us two years ago? I thought you were crazy! We knew you didn't know what you were talking about. There was no way that we would be able to influence our schools. But tonight it changed. Tonight we realized that we are doing that. We *are* influencing our friends for Christ!" Our midweek youth group hour had just ended and Kristi emerged from the overflow crowd to let me know what I already thought was true. It was true that it is God's desire for His children to be a witness for the Gospel where they are. In the case of students, that place is their school and with their friends.

A couple of years previous to this conversation, I had a very different conversation with Kristi and five other students during a Sunday school class. I had recently relocated to this church and began to work with the student ministry. When I arrived, I was surprised to learn that there was only a small group of students with an even smaller reputation in the community. I could not find anyone in their school or community who had ever heard of the church or its student ministry.

The first conversation revealed this fact and ended with this challenge: "When we are willing to follow Christ and let it be known that we are His followers, we will have an influence and impact our friends and school. I want to be a part of a student ministry like this. Will you join me?" I was met with unbelieving stares. Kristi later summarized the experience well. They thought I was crazy!

Two years later our student ministry was realizing that we actually could have an influence for Christ with our friends and in our schools. How had we come to this point? What had made the difference in the last two years? Our students began that Sunday morning to move down a road that would lead to an overflowing ministry. We put in place a strategy that was guided by several commitments for reaching their friends and influencing their schools for Christ. We committed ourselves to education, encouragement, and elevating our student ministry.

We committed ourselves to education, encouragement, and elevating our student ministry.

These commitments provided us structure, they gave us positive direction for our energy, and they helped create an atmosphere in our group and church that would be conducive to influencing our schools and making disciples of Jesus Christ. We wanted to empower our students with the desire and confidence that they could effectively reach their friends for Christ. The result of these commitments for reaching our schools was that our outlook changed, our influence changed, and we changed as we began to see what the Lord would do through us.

WE COMMITTED TO EDUCATE OUR STUDENTS

The first commitment we made in order to point our students toward reaching their school for Christ was to educate *our own students*. Education is necessary for us to show our students *why* they should be, and in fact are, witnesses. An old youth ministry principle says we should convince the students *why* they should do something and then show them *how* to do it. This principle applies when developing a program that includes evangelism.

We needed to convince students *why* it is important to share the Gospel, witness to friends at school, and stand up for Christ when they are presented with the opportunity. In convincing the students why they are to be a witness for Christ, laying a biblical foundation is the number one job for the youth worker. Then we educate them how they influence their school because of the Gospel. The Gospel is the truth of Christ and His death as payment for the penalty of our sin, His burial, and His victorious resurrection from the grave. Because of the Gospel, we know that Christ is the way to the Father. It is this dynamic truth taught to our students that will cause them to influence their school and friends for Christ.

Educate Our Students about their Direction

Matthew 28:18-20 give us the direction for our witness and influence with the Gospel. This direction is to go out with the Gospel. Jesus said to His disciples, "All authority has been given to Me in heaven and on earth. Go therefore and make disciples of all the nations, baptizing them in the name of the Father and of the Son and of the Holy Spirit, teaching them to observe all things that I have commanded you; and lo, I am with you always, even to the end of the age." We are commanded to *Go,* implying moving in a direction. The grammar of the Greek language suggests that there are several actions we are to be accomplishing while we are going. For our purpose, however, we should concentrate on going. We are to go out into the world, out of the door, out of the church, out of the safe places, and out of house. We go with the Gospel to our friends in school.

Today, many student ministries and churches, whether consciously or unconsciously, seem to teach the students to bring their friends into the church and student ministry. The idea seems to be a throwback to the old baseball movie *Field of Dreams.* The hero of the story heard a whisper from the cornfield, "If you build it, he will come," so he built a baseball diamond, his father played, and people came from all over to see the ball diamond and the game that was played on it. Like the movie, we spend a lot of time building our student ministry programs and buildings, expecting our students to bring their friends in to see it. This is not a terribly bad idea.

Ultimately, teens will come as your students reach their school for Christ. But the "you build it and they will come" idea is not the scriptural method to reach students. It begins with just the opposite idea. The students should *go* to their friends to reach them as prescribed in Matthew. Why should our students stand up for Christ? They should stand up because the Bible tells them to "Go." Go and teach the Gospel. Go and teach the Gospel to all nations, including their friends. Go and teach the Gospel to their families. Go and teach the Gospel to their schools. Go and teach the Gospel! This is the direct opposite of expecting students to bring people to your group. Teach them to *go*. Expect them to *go*! Our students' direction isn't inward, their direction is outward. It is to *go*.

> **Ultimately, teens will come as your students reach their school for Christ.**

Educate Our Students about Their Power

The second truth to teach our students comes from the Book of Acts. In verse 8 from the first chapter, Jesus says, "But you shall receive power when the Holy Spirit has come upon you; and you shall be witnesses to Me in Jerusalem, and in all Judea and Samaria, and to the end of the earth." In the book, *Pushing the Limits*, there is an extensive explanation of this passage.[1] For the purpose of educating our students, we need to highlight the truth about power that is taught in this section of Scripture.

Because our students are followers of Christ, they have the power of the Holy Spirit that will make possible their influence for the Gospel. The application of this passage for our students is that they would powerfully witness to the people closest to them. Being a witness in Jerusalem is to be a witness where our students are located, their neighborhood, and school. As we teach this concept, it should be portrayed as normal for a student who follows Christ to be a witness in the place where they live. This is their Jerusalem!

Many student ministries today put special emphasis on missions trips and foreign ministry service. While this is good in order to instill a passion for worldwide ministry, we also need to instill the vision for our Jerusalem, our friends at school, before we go to the entire world.

Our students have power to go to their schools first! We must be a witness first where Acts 1 sets the pattern for us. We must begin at home. We must go in the power of the Spirit. We must begin with our friends and classmates at school. Our students have the power of God to reach their Jerusalem, their school for Christ! It is not an impossible job; when they are followers of Christ, they already have the power!

Educate Our Students about Their Identity

Many times, our students fail in reaching their friends for Christ because those of us who teach them set them up for failure. We set the bar so high that they can't get over it. We ask them to be someone they aren't. The genius of sharing our faith at school is that the Lord never asks them to do what they cannot do and He never asks them to be someone they cannot be. John 9 tells the story of a blind man who met Jesus, was healed, and given sight. This is a wonderful report about someone who meets Jesus and then shares the story of that meeting with his family, authorities, and anyone else interested in knowing about what happened.

The man only talks about who and what he was and is. He sums up his new identity with these words found in verse 25, "One thing I know: that though I was blind, now I see." He influenced his town by talking about who he was and what he knew - his identity as a witness to the Light of the world! Our students will be successful in their influence for Christ when we educate them about their identity which is found in Christ. They can be a witness by simply talking about their own personal experience and transformation. The blind man's simple statement becomes their statement. "I was once a liar but I met Christ and now I tell the truth." "I once cheated on tests but I met Christ and now I study!" "I used to be addicted but I met Christ and now I follow Him." Our students will have an influence for Christ in their school when they know about their identity in Christ. "I don't know much else but I do know that I was blind but now I can see!"

Our students will have an influence for Christ in their school when they know about their identity in Christ.

Educate Our Students about Their Impact

We need to teach our students that they can have influence and can make an impact for Christ with their friends and in their school. There is no doubt about it, they will be successful! Why can I make this statement with so much confidence? Because Jesus has declared that we will have an impact. Matthew 5:13-16 records what Jesus said about those who are His followers: "You are the salt of the earth; but if the salt loses its flavor, how shall it be seasoned? It is then good for nothing but to be thrown out and trampled underfoot by men. You are the light of the world. A city that is set on a hill cannot be hidden. Nor do they light a lamp and put it under a basket, but on a lampstand, and it gives light to all who are in the house. Let your light so shine before men, that they may see your good works and glorify your Father in heaven."

Jesus places no limitations on the qualities of salt and light as it relates to our lives. He says we *are* salt and light. Many times we teach or at least imply that students need to try harder in order to be better salt and light. I have heard that some teach that we can do something to become better salt and light. This teaching is contrary to what Jesus is saying. We are the salt of the earth and the light of the world.

Jesus places no limitations on the qualities of salt and light as it relates to our lives.

Because our students are salt and light, they will have the impact that of salt and light has. When Jesus spoke, salt was a flavoring for food as it is today. Our students will add godly flavor to their school and culture simply by being there.

Salt was also used as an ancient preservative. It was the freezer of Jesus' day. Salt would be rubbed onto meat to slow the decay of the meat and keep it good for human consumption. When salt was present, decay was slowed. In a similar way, our students will ensure that the evil influence of their culture will be slowed. The school will be a better place simply because students who follow Christ are present!

Our students are also the light of the world. Their light will shine. People will know that our students are believers because their light shines. A lighted city on a hill cannot be hidden. The light will reflect Christ Who is in them. Because our students are salt and light, they absolutely will have these qualities and they will have an impact and influence for Christ in their school! We need to teach our students that they will have success when representing Christ. It is not what they know and say that will make the impact but it is simply who and what they are. They are salt and light. There is no doubt about their impact.

Our group needed to increase their influence and impact for Christ. In order to enable our students to reach their school, we first committed ourselves to *educate our students*. The education consisted of teaching the students about the direction of their witness, the power that is theirs when they walk into school, their identity in Christ, and the impact they can have as they are in their schools. Our students would successfully influence their schools for Christ because this education came from the Scriptures applied to their lives. They will influence their schools for Christ!

WE COMMITTED TO ENCOURAGE OUR STUDENTS

As a natural outgrowth of our students being educated, they needed to begin the process of reaching out. The second commitment for reaching the school for Christ is to encourage our students. The Scriptures say to *go* and now we must encourage them to obey. If our students were to be successful in reaching their schools for Christ, our team of adult youth workers were convinced that our encouragement would be necessary to support that success. We decided that just as it was natural for believing students to reach their friends, they must also reach them in a setting that is natural to the students. We began to encourage our students to be witnesses where they spent their time, whether in school, at home, at work, or with their friends.

Encouragement by the Presence of Adults

Encouragement first will take the form of our presence. We want our students to stand for Christ and we should be there to support them. Relationally, we ask and listen to their experiences in school. Emotionally, we build them up in case of rejection and rejoice with them in their successes. Physically, we will be there for them by supporting them in their activities when we are welcome. We will be physically there to encourage our students.

Encouragement to Interact in Class

Encouragement will also take the form of a gentle and constant prodding for them to continually move forward. Encourage our students to shine in their classes. A follower of Christ will have a point of view in virtually every course of study. We should be encouraging our students on how their faith will always interact with what they are learning. Our students should learn their assignments even if the content is divergent of biblical truth, which sometimes happens. Finally, our students must respectfully speak up when given the chance. I believe there is a balance between learning what our students are assigned, interacting with the content, and respectfully speaking up in the class and to the teacher when given the opportunity. God will bless our students when they interact in class in this way.

Encourage our students to shine in their classes.

Daniel and his three friends, Shadrach, Meshach, and Abednego, are the biblical model for this concept. They were taken prisoner by Babylon when they were about the age of some of our students. They were among the best Judah could offer and Nebuchadnezzar desired to turn them into the best Babylonians. Daniel and his friends did as they were asked. They went to class and studied for three years. They also interacted with their teachers. Because they believed in the true God, they stood up for their faith when it was appropriate and at the same time always learned what they were taught in class. At the end of the first chapter of Daniel, we are told the four of them became ten times smarter than the rest of the class. God honored them. They changed the world. We must encourage our students to do the same thing and in the same way.

Encouragement to Preserve and Shine

The fact that our students are salt and light means that there will be an impact and influence everywhere they are. We encouraged our students to be involved in other areas of their school experience. The effects of salt and light need to be felt in the school's clubs and organizations and our students need to be there. The athletic fields and teams need to be influenced for the Gospel. Extracurricular school activities should have the presence of believers. If salt and light in the form of our students is not present, evil will more quickly take control. When our students are present in all of the school activities, evil doesn't take control as the light of the world shines on the truth of Christ. We must encourage our students to impact their school for Christ and we must be there when they do.

We must encourage our students to impact their school for Christ and we must be there when they do.

WE COMMITTED TO ELEVATE OUR STUDENT MINISTRY

After I gave the initial challenge to the students on that first Sunday morning, they took the risk and began to publicly follow Christ. As leaders, we committed ourselves to help the students to reaching their school with the Gospel. When we educated our students about their mission and identity in Christ, they began to influence their school for the Gospel. They did become an influence for Christ in their school. Students began to receive Christ, they began attending church, and the group began to grow in size and influence. As this was happening, we realized that the next area of commitment would fall to the youth team. What should we be doing when students begin to become followers of Christ? As the Lord blessed us spiritually and with more numbers, the youth team members knew that we would need to *elevate our student ministry*.

Elevate Our Thinking

Most local church student ministries are busy. Many times we are considered more successful when we have more events on the calendar. Throughout the school year, some groups even schedule youth ministry events in contrast or as an alternative to the school calendar. I have seen job descriptions for youth pastors that include a minimum number of monthly youth events they would be required to plan. Because the student ministry calendar is full of church events, we demand more from our students than they have time or energy to give. Since we expect our students to reach their school for Christ, we must elevate our thinking about the volume of events we plan and the amount of activity in which we expect them to participate. We knew that our group would have to plan less activity on the corporate level so our students could do more on an individual level. We decided to have fewer events on the calendar to give opportunity for more involvement at school. The students could participate in "guilt-free" evangelism. It was guilt-free because they did not have to make choices to miss a church event in order to be effective salt and light at school and school events. We elevated our thinking about what activities we designed for our student ministry.

Elevate Our Praying

Our students needed to be both prayed for and to be praying personally. We elevated our prayer. There are tools for ministry available for the elevation of prayer and we used them. One tool, "See You at the Pole," became a yearly frame of reference for our students. At the beginning of each school year, they met at the flagpole with other students to pray for their school, country, teachers, and fellow students. Because this is a public display, it also allowed the students to stand publicly for the cause of Christ. Another prayer tool is "Harvest," sponsored by Vision for Youth. Jesus challenged His disciples to pray for more workers for the harvest of souls because the work was too big for them. Involving our students in praying for harvest workers will allow them to participate in a spiritual work that is beyond their natural experience. Change the world through prayer and the harvest of souls. Our students will also be able to apply these concepts to reaching their school.   Another vital aspect of our prayer elevation was the introduction of small groups to our student gatherings. One of our objectives in these groups was to pray for our friends at school. Each group member would submit three friends who hadn't yet met Christ personally and the group would pray for them. If a group had seven members, then twenty-one friends who were not followers of Christ were brought to the throne of grace. We prayed for our friends every week and soon it became natural that we would witness to them. The youth leaders also began to surround the students in prayer. We divided the group among ourselves and prayed for them. We also gave the names of our students to our church adults so they would pray for our students. As our group grew, so did this list. An amazing sidelight to these prayer groups was the fact that the adults in our church became very supportive of our student ministry. They prayed for the students and they backed the ministry! Elevate your praying.

Elevate Our Creativity

As already mentioned, we elevated our thinking about the calendar. As an outgrowth of this, it was time to elevate our creativity in planning the student ministry. We decided that the events that made it onto our calendar would be creative, honoring to God, biblically sound, and culturally relevant to the students. This isn't easy but it is worthwhile. Creativity would contribute to building activities that were worth the students' time. We wanted to create expectation and unpredictability in our youth meetings. Intentionally elevating our creativity forced us to do this. No youth meetings were repetitive or boring.

We devised ways to get the students involved with a view toward reaching their friends. Creative story times were used. Each week we asked for a specific number of responses to a question. For example, "Will two people tell us an answer to prayer that happened this week?"; "Will three people tell us a challenging experience this week?"; or "The first person to tell us how the Lord worked in their life this week can choose the next song for the band to lead." (We had a talented band!)

Another example of elevating our creativity was how we planned the student ministry during the month of May. May is one of the busiest months for students. They have finals, athletic events, proms, and serious preparations for the future. I promised our students that the calendar would have nothing on it besides our regular weekly student ministry meeting. Another promise was that the meeting would be worth their time. Every meeting in May would be a theme night. The first week was Tropics Night complete with a Hawaiian shirt contest and favorite Jimmy Buffet testimony song. Week two was Country and Western night when we were as corny as we could be. Every worship song had a country style, we wore cowboy hats and boots, and we sang the most famous country song ever written, *You Never Even Call Me by My Name*

Another night would be Rock and Roll night. Every worship song had a rock sound; we greased our hair and had an Elvis quiz including Elvis stuff for prizes! On the busiest month of the year for our students, the attendance increased because of elevated creativity. Finally, we used our elevated creativity to further build evangelism into the program. Most of the time, the only event on our calendar was an event we called "Friday Night Live," which was a code to our students meaning "this is an evangelism event." As members of the youth team, we made a promise to the students: the FNL would be fun, always be different, always cost two dollars (to cover food), and would always include a Gospel presentation. FNL could be on any night or day of the week but it would always include the Gospel. It was code for "bring your friends and be honest with them; tell them there will be a talk from the Bible somewhere in the program." On FNL, we did hayrides, gym nights, concerts, pool parties, volleyball tournaments, touch football, and everything else we could think up. It always would have a Gospel presentation, most of the time by our students. One other rule: if there were two FNL without unbelieving students in attendance, we wouldn't do it anymore. We always did FNL. There are students in the ministry, local church, and in education today who met Christ at a Friday Night Live. We elevated our creativity!

Kristi was correct. The Lord did bless the student ministry in our church. We did have an influence for Christ in our schools. This happened because our students took the challenge and decided to commit their lives to Christ. There were many other effects because of a growing student ministry, like service, significant ministry, and real participation in the church. It all began because we became committed to reaching our schools by educating our students, encouraging them, and elevating our program. Our students and adult youth team worked together toward influencing our schools for Christ and the Lord blessed their effort.

REVIEW QUESTIONS

1. How do you demonstrate your burden to reach unbelievers in your student ministry?

2. Where do you find students who don't know Christ or who do not attend an evangelical church in your community?

3. Do you have a plan to reach students who are not followers of Christ?

4. What measures do you take to motivate your students to reach their school for Christ?

5. How do you influence your church, outside your student ministry, to genuinely support the student ministry and students attending who may not fit the church mold?

CHAPTER 12

Making the World Smaller:
Creating a Vision for Cross-cultural Ministry

God has blessed me with opportunities to serve in short-term mission in Britain, Kazakhstan, Germany, South Africa, Mexico, Ukraine, Brazil, Columbia, Chile, South Africa, Portugal, Peru and Romania. I love learning about new cultures. I find pleasure discovering the history of a people group with whom I will serve. Many aspects of serving cross-culturally are transferable from one culture to another. Other aspects of service are unique requiring adaptation. I've learned that the more prepared you are, the more effective your ministry can be. Allow me to share some of what I've learned through pain and through joyful service.

The numbers of those taking short-term trips is growing exponentially. In 2004, Robert Priest, director of the doctoral program in Intercultural Studies at Trinity Evangelical Divinity School, reported the number could be as high as four million.[1] "Short-term mission trips (less than two weeks) are enjoying a wave of popularity with Americans eager to put faith into action and make vacations meaningful. About 1.6 million Americans took such a trip abroad last year [2005], according to a survey taken by Robert Wuthnow, Princeton University's sociologist of religion.[2] Many are going, but the question is, are they prepared?

Short-term mission experiences can be effective for teams of senders, guests, and hosts or fraught with problems. Some unwittingly damage nationals and the on-going work of career missionaries. Seth Barnes, executive director of Adventures in Missions, has guided seventy thousand people on short-term trips since 1989. He estimates that 75% of cross-cultural trips are poorly done. "Those going are increasingly ill-prepared and what they do is of questionable value given the resources invested." He goes on to say, "Participants and leaders are not being held to account by missions committees and church leaders."[3] CAM International missionary Jim Cottrill adds, "I believe that invading darkness with light is too important to take casually."[4]

"I've just returned from three months in South Africa and would love to share cultural insights, history, what to pack, and introduce you to career missionaries serving there..." This offer seemed like a god-send when my student offered to help prepare my team of ten going to South Africa. His offer was genuine and he provided valuable information about the country, its culture and people, missionaries serving there and even our first taste of South African Rooibos tea. Our cultural guide had served in a radically *different* region of the Republic of South Africa (RSA). His experience was in Durban, an area filled with poverty, violence, theft, and much physical danger. Our place of service was Capetown, one of the most affluent suburbs in all of Africa. I brought my worst clothes, when indeed I needed to have my best to minister effectively. Oops! Training for cross-cultural ministry requires more than good intentions!

Training for cross-cultural ministry requires more than good intentions!

"Would you come and teach for two weeks at Carensebes Bible Institute?" This invitation came from my long-time friend and Bible teacher, Dr. Charles Emert. At first, I resisted, knowing my inability to speak Romanian. My previous missions trips to England and later RSA allowed me to serve in English. I was filled with the fear of trying to teach interactively without knowing the language. Reluctantly, I agreed but only for one week. I discovered that love, laughter, humility, and sincerity were indeed cross-cultural languages that I could use freely. That trip changed my heart, my mind, and my life, propelling me toward career missions!

Maybe you *participated* in a mission trip as a student but *leading* a cross-cultural experience for students requires far different perspectives. The better your preparation, the greater probability your service will help and not hurt. Pre-trip team building empowers your team's effectiveness. Knowing that your intent is to help, join me in considering the prerequisites, preparation, performance, and post-trip steps for a ministry that gives God His appropriate glory.

PREREQUISITES

Six to eight months before your trip, present your pastor and missions committee your goals and possible destinations for your ministry trip. Following their final decision, schedule an informational meeting with students. Include parents and guardians when students are under age eighteen. Clearly delineate your expectations for the ministry. Clarity now will divert conflict and struggle later. Let students know, for instance, that mountain villages in Peru are primitive, so we will be living without indoor plumbing most of their time there. Know "why" you are going.

This past week, while filling out application forms for an inner-city ministry to Los Angeles, a student asked me what salvation meant! She shared that she had been baptized as an infant and had "always been a Christian." Those comments raised concerns regarding her spiritual status. Every team participant must not only have a personal faith but should learn to verbally share that *before* joining the team. How can a spiritually dead person lead others to new life in Christ? It is not unusual for students to love travel. Some need to do so for public school academic requirements. The distinctive of a church ministry trip is its spiritual work. You are not touring but sharing your life in Christ with nationals.

I encourage team members to follow Christ in baptism as a first step of obedience. In Romania, baptism and local church membership are serious matters. Romanian students face beatings, expulsion from their families and home for following Christ in baptism. If your student became a Christian as a young child, and has yet to be baptized five to ten years later, this is easily a stumbling block to national believers. For those students who are not baptized, this becomes a teachable moment rather than another "hoop to jump through." Your life example is your strongest witness!

Faithful attendance in your student ministry is foundational. A plane, train, or bus ride does not make you a missionary. I have found that those who serve most effectively at home possess more confidence in cross-cultural ministry. Attitudes of humility and submission must be evident in your student's life. You should set high but attainable standards regarding church and team meeting attendance. I meet weekly for five months to prepare my students. That time together helps forge us into a cohesive unit. I have also participated in intensive two- to three-day "boot camps" prior to leaving. Intense focused training works well especially if your students are involved in many other school or extracurricular activities.

I have found that those who serve most effectively at home possess more confidence in cross-cultural ministry.

Should every interested student participate in a cross-cultural ministry trip? My experience says "no." Written applications and individual interviews provide indicators of a student's readiness to serve. As the team leader, include youth volunteers, some mature peers, and parents on your interview team. There is wisdom in numbers and the pressure for making the decision does not fall on any one person. Here are written application questions my church uses:

1. Describe how you came to faith in Christ.

2. Where you are right now in your Christian walk? What steps are you taking to know God better?

3. Why do you desire to serve on this team?

4. What areas of ministry service have you participated in this year?

5. What spiritual gifts and natural talents and abilities do you possess that would be helpful to the team?

6. How have you demonstrated servanthood in this past year?

7. If chosen, how will you serve? Wholeheartedly, halfheartedly, apathetically?

8. Is there anything else that you would like to tell us about yourself and your desire to participate in this trip?

9. How would your parent describe your work ethic and stick-to-itiveness?[5]

Our interview questions include:

1. What are your reasons for coming on this trip?

2. How do you hope to grow on this trip?

3. What strengths and weaknesses do you feel you have? How can *you* add to our team?

4. Is there anything we should be aware of about you that will be important for us to know before allowing you to go on this trip?

5. What steps are you taking to strengthen your personal walk with God right now?

6. What must people believe to be saved from going to Hell?

7. Which Scriptures would you use to share the Gospel with someone?

8. How will you respond toward our staff, a fellow student, or the nationals when things don't go your way? (I learned this the hard way...)

Saved, baptized, serving at home, teachable spirit...these steps help in building your ministry team. Your goal is not to choose perfect students but rather those who are genuinely making steps toward maturity in Christ.

Your goal is not to choose perfect students but rather those who are genuinely making steps toward maturity in Christ.

PREPARATION

The U. S. military would never send soldiers into battle without extensive training. Likewise, we must prepare ourselves and our team for the spiritual battle that awaits us in cross-cultural service to our King of kings! As you equip your spiritual soldiers, you will be able to give account with joy as you watch for their soul (Hebrews 13:17)!

First Peter 3:15 tells believers scattered by persecution to "sanctify the Lord God in your hearts: and be ready always to give an answer to every man that asketh you a reason of the hope that is in you with meekness and fear." (KJV) It's not about arguing people into the kingdom of God. It's living so they do ask you about your hope!

Jesus prepared His followers for short-term mission trips. Luke 9 and 10 records God's training regimen. Jesus first provided His Twelve with ample authority to accomplish the work (9:1). I've accomplished this through unified Scripture reading for my team both pre-trip and in-country.

Next, Jesus defined their task as driving out demons, curing diseases, preaching the kingdom of God, and healing the sick (9:1b-2). Their ministry demonstrated through miraculous healings the authenticity of Jesus. That is not needed today because God's authority is found in His Word. While we will not be doing miracles, we will be preaching the Gospel of Christ, confronting darkness, and bringing relief to hurting people. Confusion of purpose brings discontentment, discouragement, and distraction, so make sure to review your team's task often (Proverbs 29:18).

Thirdly, short-termers were to travel light (9:3). Jesus said to leave behind extra staffs, bags, bread, money, and extra clothing as things would slow them down. A modern day equivalent would be: "leave your ipods, cell phones, fancy clothes, extra shoes at home this trip; they will distract you." Your time in country is short so stay focused. With clear instructions and limited resources, the Twelve experienced success!

Fourthly, the Twelve were to stay in the homes of those to whom they ministered. They were not to move from house to house looking for better accommodations (9:4). Living in the primitive homes of Peruvian believers in the Andes mountains made a huge life impact on my youth group. Live as close as safety will allow to nationals and watch your impact increase.

Fifthly, Jesus instructed the Twelve to shake the dust off their feet as a testimony against unbelievers who didn't receive their message (9:5). We aren't to make a scene, blow up, or leave in a huff—just move along to the next village. "So they departed and went through the towns, preaching the gospel and healing everywhere" (9:6).

Finally, the Twelve reported to Jesus their ministry's outcome. Jesus intentionally took them away with Him to recoup their strength and reflect on God's blessing: "And the apostles, when they had returned, told Him all that they had done. Then he took them and went aside privately into a deserted place (9:10)." This pattern is instructive for us.

Helping students write their salvation story will take time but will also bear much fruit. I usually have students write a rough draft comparing and contrasting their life before and after salvation, including circumstances that brought a realization of their need of a Savior. Include key Scripture verses that explain the way to Heaven as well as those that provide assurance of salvation. On one trip to eastern Europe, my team's testimony time resembled group therapy more than praise to God. I suggested but did not require each team member to share their testimony aloud before we left. Consequently they didn't receive needed feedback. Frankly, I fear those testimonies did more damage than eternal good. I had failed to caution them regarding sharing too many details of their sinful past. Had I heard testimonies pre-trip, I would have encouraged them to focus instead on the goodness and mercy of God, and Christ's sacrifice to pay the sin-debt owed.

Last summer I served alongside 120 teens in Berlin, Germany. In preparation, they memorized a number of key biblical texts. Sharing their faith through street evangelism conversations was fearful. Their available knowledge of God's truth gave them ability to answer questions that came their way. Verses like Romans 3:23; 6:23; 5:8; 10:9-10; Ephesians 2:8-9; John 1:12, 3:16, 14:6; 2 Corinthians 5:17; 1 Timothy 2:5; Hebrews 9:27; Titus 3:5-6; Acts 4:12; 2 Timothy 3:16-17: 2 Corinthians 5:21; 1 Peter 2:24 provide a strong starting point. Ask your missionary host to suggest additional texts based on the dominant religion in their field. While serving in Portugal, our hosts instructed us to describe ourselves as coming from *evangelical* Christian homes and churches since most, if not nearly all, Portuguese consider themselves "Christians."

Based on the needs of your mission focus, you will want to prepare Bible lessons, puppet skits, special musical selections both instrumental and vocal, worship songs, and devotionals by girls, biblical sermons for guys. Collegians could prepare a workshop on an aspect of the Christian life in which they have grown. Encourage practice of the ministry they will use on the field before they leave. The more they practice with children, other youth, in their home church,

Encourage practice of the ministry they will use on the field before they leave.

their neighborhood, and to other family members, the better and more confident they will become. Give constructive feedback each time they present. A ministry friend of mine requires students to play their musical instruments "around the world" (in younger age groups at church), before they play in their youth group and on a missions trip. If it's not good enough for home ministry, it's not good enough cross-culturally either.

Will you be serving where you are not fluent in the national language? Secure resources in that language. In Peru, my youth group learned songs and puppet scripts in Spanish much to the delight of our audiences! Get it right—what an insult to mangle someone's heart language! Let them know that God speaks their language.

Check the content and delivery of every song, message, testimony, and workshop with your missionary host. On one mission trip, my team unknowingly created tension between the missionaries over musical selections. This happened even after we had sung over 150 songs for our host, securing his approval. Be extra vigilant in music since you can do much damage in a short time. You don't want your missionary host repairing damage you unknowingly inflicted.

Learn as much about your host culture as possible. Youth around the world look increasingly alike on the outside, yet they possess deeply ingrained cultural differences. Ask your missionary to alert you regarding cultural differences. Listen and heed their instruction, and be ready to offer an apology as you immediately adjust your behavior. For example, students talked and laughed very loudly when riding the metro in Lisbon, calling undue attention to their American culture in a land of quiet personal relationships, which I had to address.

Some fun ways to learn about global realities involve simulation games. Serve a "World Meal" so each team member is made aware of the proportion of rice that most people around the world eat daily. Include team family members and prayer supporters too. As you realize your Western reality of overabundance, you should be humbled. The U.N. recommends 2350 calories per day. Low income countries survive on 2100 daily, middle income countries on 2700, and the US, UK, and Europe on 3700. [6]

"Dealer's Rules" simulates the frustrations and fun of learning hidden aspects of culture. Combine several distinctive sets (children's version, Disney version, etc) of UNO cards into one large deck. The dealer determines four rules and tells no one. Each time a player violates a hidden rule, the dealer hands out "punishment." A possible rule might be that each time a girl plays an even-numbered card, all the boys draw two. The game proceeds as a normal UNO game, but the goal is to discover the hidden rules. After each round of play, each player is allowed to ask the dealer one question regarding the hidden rules. Players are free to discuss among themselves their ideas. The game is over when they have guessed all the hidden rules. The dealer represents the host culture, and players are the guests or short-termers who don't know but need to discover hidden cultural rules. I take time to debrief with each team member's reaction to the frustration of living with hidden rules. [7]

Each trip I love to have a national share insight on "things to do and not do." As we drove to our game locations our first morning in Portugal, our missionary taught us five key phrases we would need. Knowing how to greet and say farewell lowered my anxiety and opened doors to Portuguese students. Practice these greetings with your team, friends, and family until you are comfortable. Eating a typical three-course Romanian meal with proper table etiquette calmed my heart for meals I would experience later.

Challenge team members to research your host culture. Learn all you can about historical events. I read three children's books on the Berlin Wall before serving in Berlin Germany. I learned that German nationals didn't want to talk about that dark episode in their past. Learn about geographical landmarks, population, dominant religious groups, form of government, names of key cities, distinctive clothing, occupations in country, exports, and so forth. Make sure you know what clothing is appropriate for church and everyday activities. In Southampton, England, the believers sit down after the final song for five minutes of silent meditation. I'm glad I knew that ahead of time. Another team I led created much misunderstanding because what was friendly behavior to them was considered seductive in our host country. Your host will inform you of what is appropriate. Listen and obey, you *don't* know more than your host!

Inform your students and their parents how much email access you will have while in-country. Select one team member to send emails reporting your safe arrival to all and an occasional group update. Your time serving is so short that you can't allow everyone personal email access. Your host will coach you regarding exchanging money at the best rate and with the least difficulty.

For your health, get necessary immunizations. South Africa suggested inoculations as if we were going to be in safari areas. We served over a thousand miles from those national parks and thus did not need the shots. Yes!

A tradition I practice is to bring hard-to-find items to my missionary host. I've carried jars of peanut butter, rolls of duct tape, bags of chocolate chips, macaroni and cheese, and seasoning packets nearly everywhere. Ask your host if you should bring crayons, balloons, copies of worksheets, and so forth or if they could be purchased more economically there. I love to leave behind with the missionary all the ministry and game equipment that I can. I've learned that leaving resources with nationals creates hurt, anger, or jealousy amongst other nationals.

Don't forget to train your senior pastor, deacons, missions committee, and financial supporters by circulating emails from your missionary. My teams spend entire training sessions literally on our knees calling out to God for our missionary hosts, their needs, our financial status, and cleansing our hearts and minds for effective service. My youth group traditionally meets the night before departure with parents and students to allow for last minute questions and emergency contact information. We end the time in rounds of concentrated prayer for our missionaries, the nationals we will serve alongside of, our students' effective service, and the calming of parental nerves! Our church commissions us prior to leaving, thus heightening the congregation's partnership in the trip.

Cross-cultural ministry drains your emotional, physical, and spiritual batteries. Start your trip at full capacity. I accomplish this by sharing socially relaxed times with my team prior to departure. I need to like my team as well as love them. My personal favorite team-building activities come from Denny Rydberg's books *Trust Builders* and *Building Community in Youth Groups* (Group Publishing). They contain 171 activities which allows you to select the right ones for your team.

Cross-cultural ministry drains your emotional, physical, and spiritual batteries.

My ministry strengths are relationships and big picture perspective. Caring for financial and secretarial details drains me mentally and emotionally. On both of my trips to South Africa, I recruited my co-leader to keep track of financial expenditures, passports, paper work, and so forth. This accentuated our strengths and freed me to focus on morale, schedule, and strategy adjustments. Recruit help for your weakness.

Flexibility is the name of short-term missions! Students need to see flexibility in you! Students need to be challenged to practice flexibility themselves! Prayer supporters need to pray for team flexibility! Team members need to keep each other alert for opportunities to practice this graceful art! It's not about *your* plan, it's about serving others!

PERFORMANCE

Once my actual journey begins, I experience a huge burden lifted from my shoulders. I need to remind myself to continue in prayerful vigilance, because my enemy Satan would like nothing more than for me to drop my guard and proceed to battle without full protection (Ephesians 6: 10-20).

I like to have my team reading the same devotional book while on our mission. This helps build a spirit of oneness. My high school staff prepares journals and Scripture reading for each day to encourage students to record their impressions and growth. Setting aside time daily for this exercise is essential to its completion; students do what you make time for, not what you suggest. Set the example for daily time with God.

How you end one day significantly affects how the next day begins. I like to end each day with team prayer and reflection on lessons learned and victories won. During one Romania trip, we met each evening after campers were sleeping to share positives of our teammate's actions. This kept us affirming and not picking at one another. Serving while immersed in the Portuguese language without hardly any knowledge of the language heightened my team's frustration level. To combat this I planned intentional times away from the ministry site for personal refreshment. We didn't go far—just up the hill behind the camp—but that did help us to refocus. As team leader, I work hard to be intentionally more flexible, positive, affirming, and encouraging to students. Students are aware of their short-comings. My goal is to correct inappropriate behavior only with those involved. When I correct the whole group, the guilty person often misses the correction and the tenderhearted student is overwhelmed with false guilt. Redirecting inappropriate behavior maximizes teachable moments. Students are beginners, not experts. I remind myself to be realistic while encouraging growth.

POST TRIP

Jesus set a clear example for us when He regathered the Twelve in Luke 9:10. They reported what they had accomplished in nearby towns. Good cross-cultural trips likewise rehearse victories small and great.

Jesus' re-entry model intentionally planned time for physical and emotional refreshment. He retreated with them to a solitary place after their return. My youth group plans a photo party for a week or two after the trip when everyone gathers to share photos and memories.

One adult makes available a CD with a trip video and selected digital photographs priced to cover the materials. We celebrate as we review and laugh together.

My personal weakness in cross-cultural missions is re-entry and debrief. I give everything in service to the point of physical, emotional, and spiritual exhaustion. I don't say that to my praise but rather as an admission that I need to change. I am working to practice the truth that life lessons come most easily after thoughtful reflection prompted by guided conversation. Some good questions for reflection are in International Mission Board's (IMB) Moving On - exercise (see Appendix A).[8] As your trip draws to a close, encourage your students to consider what they've learned. If I don't make time to reflect on my ministry, I was busy but missed growing.

Help your students share meaningfully about their experiences. One mom mentioned how much she appreciated seeing my pictures of a cross-cultural trip. Her son primarily took pictures of the missionary's two dogs and not much else! A Christian school near me plans a post-trip meal with family members to share spiritual lessons learned. Present the outcome of your trip to the entire student group to keep them connected. Seth Barnes suggests preparing a sixty-second version, three-minute version, and twenty-minute church presentation to answer the question "How was your trip?"[9] Seth also lists thirty debriefing questions (see Appendix B).[10] I mail a one-page summary of my trip's blessings to every prayer and financial supporters. Help your student do the same. Finally, one or two months after your students have returned from their mission trip, have your students reflect again on the effect their trip had on their lives. The Settling Back In exercise from IMB is an excellent tool to use for this purpose (see Appendix C).[11]

Help your students share meaningfully about their experiences.

PRODUCTIVITY

Are you overwhelmed with the amount of preparation necessary for a maximized trip? I've felt that myself many times. My suggestion is to do all that you reasonably can. You won't be perfect your first trip. Begin modestly and grow as a leader each time. Recruit others to help you at every stage. Consider your church secretarial staff, mission committee members, parents, and students as partners. We serve an excellent God, so let's represent Him that same way! I'm not an expert in cross-cultural training, but God has used my humble efforts to call several to career missions in the very countries where I first took them. Is it worth the effort? Absolutely. It is worth any effort I have invested. God will honor your investment too.

REVIEW QUESTIONS

1. State the purpose for your cross-cultural experience in one sentence.

2. Does your cross-cultural experience meet the needs of your missionary host and nationals?

3. Whom have you recruited to assist you in training your team? What will each person bring to the team? Music ability, drama expertise, Bible teaching abilities, sermon prep know how, building skills, and so forth?

4. What is some potential damage to nationals and missionaries if your team arrives unprepared in heart? Mind? Body? Spirit? Emotion?

5. How will you find potential places to serve: with mission agencies in which you have confidence? With missionaries your church supports? With an organization that specializes in STM (short-term missions)?

6. How will you determine the success of your trip? When does the cost outweigh the benefit?

CHAPTER 13

It's Their Church Too:
Serving in the Local Church

"What seems to help your youth grow more than anything else?" I asked.

The answer was, "When the students went on some short-term mission trips; they came back excited, walking with God, and were motivated to follow Him."

Then why not have a mission trip every week?

Obviously, that can't happen, but why are our students not involved in ministry all the time? Ministering for the cause of Christ is the greatest catalyst for spiritual growth that a student can experience.

As a youth worker, you are a coach. You are to be the one who is equipping a team of students to be successful in winning the game of life. Coaching a sport parallels what a typical youth worker does in the local church.

As a youth worker, you are a coach. You are to be the one who is equipping a team of students to be successful in winning the game of life.

If you were coaching a basketball team, you would need to do the following:

1. *Demonstrate* how to be an effective basketball player.

2. *Equip the team* by having *practices*, workouts, and strength training.

3. You would *motivate* them.

4. You would *not be permitted to play* in the game yourself. You are only to equip them.

5. You are responsible for *scheduling the games*. If you don't schedule enough games, you would soon discover that your team would lose heart.

We see the importance of the role of a coach in a sport yet we do not see the similarity as it relates to coaching students in a local church. There needs to be regular opportunities for the students to put their Christianity into practice. A parallel exists between a youth worker and a sports coach. The question, however, remains as to whether we schedule enough opportunities for them to "play." Do we motivate and train students only to give them few opportunities to play? Helping students serve God is a key role youth workers much embrace. It is when students serve others that they are serving the Lord. We can see that in 2 Corinthians 9:12-13 or Matthew 20:27-28 or through the implications of Matthew 25:37-40.

1. Issues We Face in Challenging Youth to Service in the Local Church

a. Wrong concept of youth ministry. It is possible for churches to have a "baby-sitting" emphasis on youth until they become adults, rather than motivating them to serve now.

I know of a large, growing church that had an interview process developed to find a new youth pastor. Members of the committee were making contacts with potential youth workers when one of the men being interviewed pointed out that the church had an incorrect approach to youth work. It was written that the church "has a ministry to students." The prospective youth pastor carefully pointed out that the statement should read that the church has a ministry "of" students, not "to" students. There is a major difference. One approach sees students as people who are served; the other approach shows that youth are there to serve.

b. **Youth are isolated.** As churches attempt to put a needed emphasis on young people, they sometimes inadvertently segment the youth from the rest of the body of believers. In the small church where there are volunteer youth workers, this is not as common as it is in the larger churches. When a youth ministry grows it often develops such separate programs that the rest of the church is isolated from the students. This is not healthy. First Corinthians 12 points out that all believers are important in the body of Christ. Verses 12 and 13 emphasize that all believers are important in the body of Christ.

There are two types of leadership the young people can have within the church: 1) They can be leaders in the youth group or; 2) They can be used within the church *beyond* the scope of the youth ministry. I believe the best approach is when youth are used in areas beyond the youth ministry. I like to see youth greeting people, working in the nursery, singing on the worship team, doing ushering, reading Scripture, giving tithes and offerings, helping the church office, visiting, discipling, running sound, and participating in church work days.

When youth are not engaged with people beyond the youth ministry, they become so isolated that they know few adults beyond those who work with the youth ministry. And when they graduate from high school (or sooner) they could easily leave the church. They do not feel that the whole church is theirs.

To solve this is not only to work at intergenerational ministries but by church leaders showing respect for the young people. The U.S. government will allow an eighteen-year old to fly a multi-million dollar jet. If the government trusts young people with major responsibilities, the church must allow youth to do more than occasionally take up the offering.

c. We over-inform students before we use them. Sure, teaching is important. But I think most of our churches err in giving far too much information compared to giving students projects to do. Most people learn best by doing, not listening.

Dr. Mark Senter says, "Perhaps the greatest hindrance to rapidly moving young people into ministry postures is the myth of 'know before do.' We give too much information compared to giving students the opportunities to live out what they know."[1] A student learns to play football by going outside on a field and throwing around a football. A student learns to drive by getting behind the wheel of a car. Someone will never learn to swim without getting into the water. Teaching is important; I just think we err in not giving our students enough opportunities to live out what we are teaching.

We also cannot buy into the myth that says that if we "teach" the truth, people will automatically do it. Many times a person will be motivated to listen to the teaching *after* he or she has learned why it is important.

James 1:22 warns us that it is possible to deceive ourselves into believing that we are "doing" Christianity just because we are hearing it. When we hear the Word over and over, I believe we can actually think we are "doing" it and we are totally incorrect. James says, "But be doers of the word, and not hearers only, deceiving yourselves."

Jesus modeled the need for getting His followers "out" right away. He did not over-inform them. In fact, the disciples were probably scared to death, but He sent them out right away. He did not wait until they knew everything. He sent them with a command and told them to go ahead of Him and He sent them two by two.

I find it interesting that Jesus, when He had chosen the Twelve, sent them out. Luke 9:1-2 states, "Then He called His twelve disciples together and gave them power and authority over all demons, and to cure diseases. He sent them to preach the kingdom of God and to heal the sick."

In a similar passage in Luke 10:1-3, He seemed to send them out immediately after they had been appointed.

After these things the Lord appointed seventy others also, and sent them two by two before His face into every city and place where He Himself was about to go. Then He said to them, "The harvest truly is great, but the laborers are few; therefore pray the Lord of the harvest to send out laborers into His harvest. Go your way; behold, I send you out as lambs among wolves."

In verse 17 of that chapter, they returned with both joy and power! The point is, like the sports coach, we are responsible to schedule the games, not just train them.

d. **We misapply the concept of ministry—whatever "that" is!** We have too few words in the English language for the word *ministry*. We use ministry for everything. It ranges from being a pastor or missionary to sports ministry with the church softball team. Are they all ministries? Yes...if they are done with the right spirit—to serve the Lord—but believe me there is a huge difference between a student who is a youth group usher and a student who is working hard to share his faith at school.

Ministry is so broad that it becomes confusing to everyone. Then on top of all that, we have wrongly made the cross-cultural experience the "ultimate" ministry. While I love seeing students go on mission trips, I do not see that as an end in itself. I think it is easier for them to share Christ in a new culture with groups unlike themselves, than it is for them to share Christ with the student who sits next to them in band at school.

We have wrongly made the cross-cultural experience the "ultimate" ministry.

We can use short-term mission experiences to train students to bring it back home, but that is where it counts—back home. If they can love another culture and share Christ there, I hope the student will bring it back.

Youth ministries can become "far-sighted." A far-sighted person needs to have his eyes corrected because he can see clearly at a distance but cannot see up-close. The same could happen with a missions experience. "Although ministry in another culture or country may be exciting and appealing to high-schoolers, ministry to non-believing peers in a local community requires far more spiritual maturity,"[2] says Dann Spader, the founder of Sonlife Ministries.

Let me be quick to say that short-term mission experiences are good. I like them and encourage students to participate; however I feel that they should not get our primary attention. The student who shares Christ regularly with his peers at school really needs the publicity—not just reports from overseas.

I know of a church that had a missions conference; a girl in eleventh grade made a decision to be a "missionary" as a result of the emphasis. When asked where she wanted to go, she said, "To the public school." She was in a Christian school and she felt it was time for her to apply her Christianity. Her parents allowed her to enroll in the public school. She was able to be such a testimony that almost every week she brought non-Christian kids from her school to the church. They even put her picture up with the other church missionaries posted on the church walls and had prayer groups for her. She became used of God to reach a number of friends for Christ. Now that is balance—blessing the youth who live it now.

Years ago, I benefitted from a chart of ministry levels. This chart, developed by the people at Sonlife Ministries, was so helpful to me. It demonstrated various levels of ministry. While all are "ministries," it clearly shows the difference between a task-ministry and a people-ministry. It also shows the difference between doing it as a project and doing ministries over the long-haul. I have adapted the chart and you will find it at the end of this chapter.

e. **We do not expect students to serve in our church yet.**
Today's students have placed school above church. As a result, youth ministries have capitulated to the pressure and

we do not challenge the students to serve. We need to show the students that the church wants them and needs them. I also feel we need to challenge the students to belong to the church. It is their church. When you have a youth retreat, do not only call for commitments to Christ, but call for follow-up. If we believe the church is God's program, we should be urging students to be baptized publicly. We need to call them to become church members, to tithe, to serve, to cut back on some of their extra-curricular activities in order to serve in the church. Set up examples of adults in your church who have made sacrifices to be at church and to serve the Lord.

But what about these students who are in dramas and sports at school? Don't fight it; celebrate it. Ask the guy who is going out for football if he will do it as a ministry of the church? Ask if you can pray for him and ask him how he intends to use football as a means of serving the Lord and representing the church and youth group. Then have him report to the youth ministry as to how things are going in his outreach there. Add his name to your youth group prayer list. This same thing applies to students who take jobs. Call them in to ask if they would take this job as a ministry, not just a place to get money. Help them think through ways they could serve the Lord. Give them ideas such as: bringing a Bible to work to read on breaks, being a great example of a diligent, hard worker, using God-talk, targeting one or more employees to befriend and pray for, or even tithing to the church. Tell them you would like to meet with them on occasion so they feel your support and love.

2. Creating an Atmosphere Where Youth Will want to be Involved in Church.

I am disturbed that more youth say they are believers (they pray and even read their Bibles) but they just do not want to be involved in church. They see the church as being irrelevant to their needs and question why they need to feel "guilt-tripped" into being in church. My own experience is that this attitude is not only present but that it is far too prominent.

I urge youth workers to do random interviews with students in your community and ask them about their beliefs, if they go to church, and why or why not. It will open your eyes to the needs of your students and church. Too often we think we are doing just fine, but we have only questioned the people who are inside the walls of our church. The facts you receive might startle the local church and help create avenues to reach students who are not engaged in the church.

a. **Help believing students see the dynamic of the local church.** It could be that we are our own worst enemy. We need to verbalize the value of the local church. Quit comparing your church to other churches. First and foremost, we need to teach that God is the head of the church. The church is His idea and He wants us to be connected to the local body of believers. Consider verses like Matthew 16:18 when Christ says, "I will build My church, and the gates of Hades shall not prevail against it." Look at Ephesians 1:22 and passages like Colossians 1:18-20 or Hebrews 10:24-25.

I would encourage youth workers to discuss the strengths of a local body (all ages, all walks of life, prayer partners, accountability, Bible teaching, discipleship, a sense of family, a place to serve, where you call for counseling, marrying, burying, sickness, and so forth). Let the students recognize the uniqueness of a church. Help them also see the varieties of types of churches, from one culture to another in the world or in societies (styles of music, house churches, high-brow churches, African American churches, service times, buildings). Explain the differences of churches in whether they are really a part of God's church or not—liberal groups, churches who do not believe the Bible is inerrant, and so forth. Help the students value what they like about your church. Help them think of people they like and help them see God in the church.

b. **Connect students with all ages of church members, especially leaders.** Teach the students that the church is like a family and that we need each other. We especially need to have teachable attitudes to learn from other people. Luke 6:40 explains that the examples of those with whom we associate are what God uses to help us have godly character. "A student is not above his teacher, but everyone who is fully trained will be like his teacher." (Luke 6:40 NIV).

Help the students see the value to being connected with adults in the church. Work at making the church intergenerational. The students need the adults and the adults are commanded to teach the younger. Help them make this a reality. By all means, try not to separate the youth from the rest of the church in celebration services. The students will not learn to know the adults if students are too separated.

c. **Expose students to the potential of their local church.** Showing the students what their church is doing and exposing them to what "could" happen not only gives vision, but could implant desire to serve in the their church.

> *Showing the students what their church is doing and exposing them to what "could" happen not only gives vision, but could implant desire to serve in the their church.*

One way to do that is to have "windshield tours" of areas of your community. Take the students in a van or bus and show them various sections of the city and pray for workers to reach those people. It could be to an apartment complex, or to where kids often play, to an ethnic community, to a homeless part of town, or.... At each place have students pray that God will supply people who will reach these people for Christ. Remember that Jesus calls on us to pray for workers for the harvest fields in Matthew 9:35-38. We should stimulate interest among the youth to try to reach various groups in the community. Help the students identify students in their school who are international students. They are especially in need of friendships and many need to know Christ.

Taking the youth to see various ministries can be great for stimulating students to see that God could use them to reach people for Christ now. By showing youth they can make a difference, it reminds them that the best people to reach students for Christ are other students.

d. **Create an expectation that youth are to serve, not just receive.** I believe one way to teach this is to explain that many leaders in the Bible were probably young people themselves. Mary and Joseph were probably not yet twenty years old. So were most of the apostles. They were still able to reach out to others.

Encourage students to know that they are needed in the body of Christ. Teach them from 1 Corinthians 12 that there are many spiritual gifts that are to be used to serve others. We learn our gifts by serving others. Students need to begin doing ministries to see where it is that God has gifted them.

Doug Fields in *Purpose-Driven Youth Ministry* uses a resource called SHAPE. It is an acrostic for Spiritual gift, Heart, Ability, Personality, and Experience. By giving these tests, he helps students determine where they would most like to serve God.[3]

Expect the students to serve others. Encourage them to be the greatest "givers" in the church. Use passages like 1 Thessalonians 1:1-10 as a Bible study and help them see that the worst example they could be to the church would be to be "takers, not givers." It is more blessed to give than to receive.

We should point out that students are crucial to the vitality of the church and if they are bad examples they can ruin the testimony of the church. I love 1 Timothy 4:12 as a reminder that no one should look down on them because they are young, but they should be positive examples of what they want believers to be.

Note: It has been my experience that students need training on how to be respectful to people and how to begin conversations and keep them going. They can say "hi" and get general information, but after that they don't know what to do.

3. How to Train Students to Serve God Through the Church

a. **Start with focusing on children's ministries, not just youth ministries.** Encourage children to volunteer to set up chairs, to befriend another child, and to share Jesus with their school friends. We may have overlooked the fact that if children are old enough to receive Christ, they can also lead other children to Christ. Here is a list of other examples of how to get children involved in serving:

1. Teach them how to operate the sound for children's church.

2. Start a worship team for children.

3. Use children in special music.

4. Assign children to memorize (or read) the Scripture for the next week.

5. Challenge children to explain where they were when they asked Jesus into their life and why they received Christ. Then ask them to share their testimony with someone during the week.

6. Use children in grades four to six to be involved in "mission trips" to a nursing home, urban ministry, rescue mission, or a cross-cultural group. Children can do puppets, sing, share verses, or visit with people.

7. Ask the children to make cookies for camp or VBS.

8. Consider having a program of children's Bible quizzing to show to the church.

9. Urge the adults to use the children's church service on occasion to read Scripture, lead in prayer, sing a special number, or share the verse of the month.

b. **Give the students ownership of the youth ministry so that they share the burden.** Through the years I have seen youth workers doing too much of the ministry themselves. If we do not give more ownership to the students, then they will learn to be followers, not leaders. It is healthy for the students feel the sense of ownership for what is happening in the youth ministry.

Allow students to make mistakes. I am reminded that Jesus allowed the disciples to do many things without His being there. Sometimes they failed, but they usually returned more teachable. One passage I relate to this is in Matthew 16:5-7 when they forgot to take the bread. There were times when they argued among themselves or couldn't heal someone even though Jesus had given them the power to do it. Then there was Peter's walking on the water and beginning to drown or his denial of Jesus. In fact, Jesus even allowed for Judas Iscariot to be in the group. The disciples learned by doing and Jesus was nearby to help them up if they were willing to change.

There is a difference between the words *teach* and *equip*. Teaching is more didactic while equipping is more learning by doing. I believe if we will equip students to do and give them projects to do with assignments and accountability, it will help the students more than expecting them to do what is right. We have all heard the statement, "We do not do what is expected; we do what is inspected." We need to release segments of the youth ministry to the students and help them be successful.

Let students take ownership under these guiding principles:

1. As a youth leader, you are delegating a segment of the ministry to them. Final decisions are yours. A delegated authority is not a relinquished authority. You can veto or question a decision because you are the one held responsible by the church body.

2. Always explain the need to clear decisions with you relating to finances, image, liability, and spiritual direction.

3. Make all your delegations a spiritual decision. Even when I let the students plan the games I asked them to meet in my office to approve the games and I reminded them that games are for relationship-building and encouragement and that games must be explained carefully. I then ask him what games he will play and how he will approach it. I always pray with the student.

4. If the student is new or inexperienced, don't delegate as much. For the students that you trust, I would give them much bigger responsibilities—even overseeing a puppet team ministry or discipling a group of younger students.

5. I have no problem with allowing students who are not yet believers to help with some elements of the task-oriented ministries.

6. Always use the ministries as an opportunity to encourage the students by verbal and printed appreciation. Encourage students to acknowledge and thank any who serve in the church.

Depending on the spiritual level of the students, the involvement could range from simple tasks such as painting something or doing photography, to letting students lead youth talks or overseeing a youth retreat.

In order to encourage more student involvement, why not use your students as interns for your youth ministry? I have attached a sample way to train students in church ministry by using them as "Summer Servants," found in Appendix D.

c. **Equip the students to serve the Lord by serving others.** Students know the difference between "performance" and "heart-felt ministry." I would help them see the differences by explaining how crucial it is to have students who serve the Lord and are not serving for the applause of others.

1. Schedule group events outside the church. As I mentioned earlier, one role of a sports coach is to schedule games. Keep students involved in ministries inside and outside the church. Going on ministry trips as a youth group is very helpful. Go to a nursing home and help them connect with the people and build relationships. Evaluate afterwards and commend the students who are willing to reach out even when it might have been uncomfortable. Schedule weekend ministries to nearby churches. Sponsor a puppet team trip to four or five places one Saturday. Go to urban centers, Appalachia, or cross-cultural ministries outside the United States. The key is bringing it back home to win their friends to Christ.

2. Schedule Youth Sundays to feature the young people in music, testimonies, dramas, speaking, or worship bands to give them an opportunity to serve locally.

3. Use students in a variety of ways in the church such as nursery work, ushering, teaching children, and so forth. Since youth are a part of the church I like using them in all kinds of ministries. It may be beneficial to use youth for short-term projects even if it takes them temporarily out of the youth group. They need a variety of experiences so they can learn their spiritual gifts and still remain connected to the youth group.

4. Teach church involvement. I would encourage youth ministries to teach the value of giving tithes and offerings as a form of worship. To stimulate this concept you could have a youth group offering project that the youth collect separately and give as a unit to the local church. That way it is possible to monitor the giving of students more closely. Giving to the Lord's work is part of getting students involved in their local church. Don't forget that Scripture teaches: "For where your treasure is, there your heart will be also," (Matthew 6:21). If students will willingly give to the local church, their hearts will be drawn there as well. Remember the order of the verse. If a person gives, his heart will follow—not the opposite.

5. Consider a ministry development incentive program. Such programs are available from denominational or para-church organizations. For example, Word of Life has a program called Teens Involved, or Bible Quizzing. A program we use at CE National is called NAC—Nurturing Abilities for Christ. It is an incentive program like many others that include Bible quizzing and categories in vocal music, instrumental music, interpretive music, oratory skills, or original works such as writing, art, and media. It stimulates involvement and allows youth to be "judged" and encouraged.

6. Connect students with adults in the church. As a youth sponsor you are to work yourself out of a job. You are to connect students to others in the body of Christ. This is not just a good idea, I believe it is an essential part of what must happen in a youth ministry.

It is imperative that we help connect students with parents as well. The parents should be the primary spiritual caregivers in their lives. We only supplement the home.

Building bridges to the local church within our youth ministry is essential. If we establish a large youth ministry and never see the youth involved with the rest of the local church, then we are disillusioned as to success. Serving in the local church can help establish a foundation for their lives, and we want to be an intricate part of their lives now and in the future.

REVIEW QUESTIONS

1. Meet with several young people and church leaders to evaluate how the youth are involved in the church as a whole. Is there something you should be doing to help the students connect with the church in a greater way? What steps should you choose?

2. Are the children (elementary and above) involved in the church? What can you do to keep a consistent flow between children and youth? Is this continuing on to high school graduates? Are you losing students from the church after they graduate from high school?

3. Evaluate the following: do you have a ministry to youth or of youth? Would the community see your youth ministry as "reaching out"? Have you identified students who are at the top levels of the ministry chart? Who should you especially nurture?

4. Would incentive programs help your youth be more involved in ministries? Do you need to get students working on NAC, Bible Quizzing or Teens Involved (Word of Life)?

5. Evaluate how you are equipping students to feel that the church is theirs. Consider the following: using youth in the overall church ministries; using youth in church services; tithing; doing outreach into the community; developing leadership from the youth; and encouraging the youth and youth leaders.

MINISTRY CHART:
WHERE MINISTRIES ARE NOT ALL THE SAME

Ministry Levels	Duration	What?	Description	Example
One	Short-term	Task	Performing a task that does not involve a great deal of deep interaction with people	Rake leaves, be an usher, do a website, type, paint, clean, greet, hand out fliers
Two	Short-term	Person unlike you	Doing any type of ministry (task, shepherding, love, outreach) to an age-group or culture that is not your own	Nursery worker, rescue mission, senior citizen home, overseas cross-cultural ministry to another people group
Three	Short-term	Peer	Doing any type of ministry (task, love, shepherding, outreach) to your own peer group	Reaching, teaching, or discipling your peers at school, neighborhood, church, community
Four	Long-term	Task	Performing on-going tasks that do not involve a great deal of deep interaction with people	Being "servants" to others by regularly serving as sound or video technicians, parking lot attendants, greeters, website developers, worship team members
Five	Long-term	Person unlike you	Doing any type of on-going ministry (task, shepherding, love, outreach) to an age-group or culture that is not your own	Being regularly involved in ministries to children, senior adults, people in jail, or being a foreign missionary in another language group
Six	Long-term	Peer	Doing any type of on-going ministry (task, love, shepherding, outreach) to your own age group	Regularly sharing Christ with your peers. This can involve reaching people like yourself—students at school, sports teams, clubs
Seven	Long-term	Always being "on mission"—especially with your peers	Doing on-going ministries that involves fulfilling goals of intentionally reaching and discipling people—especially your peers	Regularly and intentionally sharing Christ with people like yourself. This could be neighbors, school friends, and so forth through a strategic attempt to be "on mission" always

CHAPTER 14

No-Guilt Recruiting:
Steering Students toward Vocational Ministry

There are over six and a half billion people in the world today. That number will reach seven billion by 2012 and eight billion by 2025! I have no idea what the world population statistics looked like when Jesus walked the face of this earth, but I do know that He was very concerned about the great number of people who needed a Savior. Early in His ministry with the disciples, He challenged them to "open your eyes and look at the fields" because "they are ripe for harvest" (John 4:35 NIV). Jesus was moved with compassion by the multitudes that needed a shepherd and He wanted His disciples to have the same burden for people that He did.

Dr. Michael Loftis, president of the Association of Baptists for World Evangelism, compared the world's population with the annual world-wide conversion statistics and came up with an eye-opening figure. 124,000,000 people are born every year without Christ. It is estimated that missionaries from evangelical mission agencies baptize about 4,000,000 converts per year.[1] When you subtract the number of converts per year from the number of births per year, you are left with 120,000,000 people *each year* who still need Jesus Christ. Does that open your eyes?

But Jesus wasn't only concerned about the size of the harvest; He was equally concerned that there were not enough workers willing to go into the harvest. When He told His disciples to open their eyes, He

Jesus wasn't only concerned about the size of the harvest; He was equally concerned that there were not enough workers willing to go into the harvest.

not only wanted them to see the harvest, He wanted them to do something about it! In fact, His words to the disciples were, "The harvest is plentiful but the workers are few. Ask the Lord of the harvest, therefore, to send out workers into His harvest field," (Matthew 9:37-38 NIV) and in Matthew 10 He proceeded to send out the twelve disciples to preach to the nation of Israel.

The average person sitting in church today would most likely believe that the United States sends more missionaries overseas than any other country in the world. They may conclude that we can always do better, but compared with the rest of the world, we're doing a pretty good job. If that's what you believe, your thinking is inaccurate. In the late 1980's, America ranked sixteenth per capita in the list of countries sending missionaries overseas[2] and the situation hasn't improved. After documenting the growth of the church around the world, Dave Livermore, in his excellent book, *Serving with Eyes Wide Open*, addresses the need, not just for missionaries, but for workers to serve around the world, when he says, "Seven thousand new church leaders are needed daily to care for the growing church," and concludes, "A realistic perspective on the realities of the global church has to include the huge need for equipped ministry leaders."[3] It is obvious that the need for workers is greater than it has ever been!

I could continue to quote statistic after statistic about the size of the harvest around the world and the lack of believers committed to doing anything about it, but if you do not feel the heartbeat of Jesus as described in Matthew 9 and John 4, these statistics are nothing more than meaningless numbers. There's no doubt that Jesus' words are truer today than when He uttered them over two thousand years ago. So the question that ought to haunt the church today is, "What are we going to do about the great harvest and the few workers willing to go out into the harvest"?

Please remember Jesus' concluding statement that we pray for the Lord of the harvest to send out workers into His harvest field. Prayer must be the first thing we do if we expect to find the needed workers for the harvest. If we are serious about our students becoming the next generation of workers committed to reaching our world, we must also get serious about asking God to send them out of our homes, churches, youth ministries, Christian schools, camps, and Christian colleges to serve Him in full-time, vocational, career, or as Woodrow Kroll calls it, "lifetime ministry"![4]

In a day when many churches are canceling prayer meeting or have turned it into another church service with a ten minute prayer time at the end, we must emphasize prayer as the first and foremost activity necessary to see our students called into lifetime ministry. At a time when local church youth ministries are being evaluated as to the relevancy of their programs to the lives of their students, it is imperative that we teach our students that prayer is one of the most relevant activities in which they can participate. In fact, there are few things that are more relevant to understanding God's purpose for their lives than that they give themselves to serious prayer about the possibility of lifetime ministry. If we believe that prayer is the answer, we must pray regularly, consistently, urgently, confidently, and expectantly that God will send our students as laborers into His harvest!

There are few things that are more relevant to understanding God's purpose for their lives than that they give themselves to serious prayer about the possibility of lifetime ministry.

However, there is more that we can do to be part of God's plan to send workers into the harvest. We must also change the way that we think about lifetime ministry. In John 4, Jesus told the disciples that they must change the way they were thinking about the work of God and the needs of people.

The disciples were thinking about food, one of their favorite pastimes, and wanted Jesus to eat something. He responded with, "I have food to eat of which you do not know," (v. 32) and the disciples, completely missing the point, wondered if someone had already brought Him a snack. And then Jesus made His point, "My food is to do the will of Him who sent Me, and to finish His work" (v. 34). The thing that nourished Him, the thing that satisfied His soul, and the thing that burned in His heart was to finish the work that God had sent Him to earth to accomplish! He wanted that same sense of urgency about God's work to burn in the disciples' hearts, so He again challenged their thinking by telling them to open their eyes and look at the harvest. They didn't have to wait for the typical four-month interval between sowing and reaping; people were everywhere, they were coming to Jesus, and they were ripe for the harvest!

The local church is at the heart of God's plan to reach the world and must be the place where the change in thinking about the need for workers begins. When is the last time you heard any mention of the great need for workers to reach the harvest? When is the last time you heard a message from your pastor, or for that matter, any speaker about the need of workers for the harvest? When is the last time you heard anyone challenge the students in your church to give their lives to lifetime ministry? If you are involved in youth ministry, when is the last time you encouraged the parents in your church to talk to their kids about seriously considering a career in lifetime ministry? When is the last time you asked a student if he had ever thought about serving God with his life? When is the last time you asked God to send students from your church into the harvest? Have I made my point?

If I could sit down and discuss this matter with you, your response to all of these questions might be, "It has been a long time," or, "I can't remember the last time." And then in your own defense you might add, "But I'm not opposed to students going into lifetime ministry, I just haven't thought much about it!" And that is precisely the problem. Not many believers are thinking about the great harvest and even fewer about the need for workers. For most people, lifetime ministry is rarely thought about, let alone talked about in the auditoriums, classrooms, or hallways of our churches!

I have served in lifetime ministry for over thirty-three years as a pastor, youth pastor, and an administrator at a Bible college whose mission has been to equip men and women for careers in ministry. I recognize that at this time in the life of the church, there are no easy answers or overnight solutions to significantly increase the number of workers willing to go into the harvest. However, I believe we can develop a strategy that will change the thinking of God's people and ultimately the ministry-mindedness of our churches.

I grew up in Cherry Hill, New Jersey, just across the Delaware River from Philadelphia and became an avid Philadelphia sports fan. You got it—the "City of Brotherly Shove." Our fans are sometimes referred to as the "Boo-birds" because they'd rather boo than cheer, except of course, when a player from the other team gets hurt. That's right; you got a problem with that?! Just kidding. That means my favorite teams are the Phillies, the Eagles, the 76ers, and the Flyers.

After graduating from high school, I spent a year at Temple University in Philadelphia studying architecture before I transferred to a small Bible college in the Midwest. I graduated, got married, and after a couple of years as the pastor of a small church in southern Iowa, became the youth pastor at a church just south of Chicago.

While we lived in the Chicago area, our three children were born (two boys and a girl), the Bears won a Super Bowl, Michael Jordan was drafted by the Bulls, and the Cubs, as usual, were telling their fans to "wait until next year!" You might think that my boys would have grown up cheering for the Chicago teams. But with the exception of a couple of Bears jerseys and a few Michael Jordan pictures, that didn't happen. After moving to northeastern Pennsylvania for their junior high, high school, and college years, Luke and John became Philadelphia fanatics just like their Dad.

By now you might be asking why anyone cares how my boys and I became fans of the Philadelphia sports teams and what this has to do with changing the ministry tone and thinking of our churches or raising up a whole new generation of workers for the harvest. I'm glad you asked, but I'm not ready to explain it yet, so hang in there.

I also want to tell you about my Aunt Priscilla, who until she went home to Heaven last year, had lived in East Lansing, Michigan for over fifty years. She was a huge fan of the Michigan State University Spartans. I have pictures of me as a baby wearing a Michigan State t-shirt and matching shorts. I grew up wearing green and white and it wasn't long before I was also cheering for MSU. As my boys grew up, Aunt Priscilla outfitted them with t-shirts, sweatshirts, hats, and all kinds of stuff from Michigan State and as you might imagine, Luke and John became Spartan fans.

So what's the deal?! What's the point of these Philadelphia and Michigan State stories? The point is that I never once told Luke or John that they had to cheer for any of these teams, nor did I threaten them with bodily harm or starvation if they chose to like other professional or college teams. I didn't expose them to brainwashing or psychological manipulation of any kind and yet, they still became followers of "my" teams. It's real simple: for years they watched the games I watched and talked about the players and teams that I talked about and wore the same team stuff that I did. They loved their Dad and like boys do, they liked the things Dad liked and wanted to do the things that Dad did. Because I was excited about the Philadelphia Eagles, they were excited about the Philadelphia Eagles. Because I was excited about Michigan State, they were excited about Michigan State.

ARE YOU STILL WITH ME?

I'm sure my analogy might break down for some fathers and sons. Maybe it's NASCAR or music or woodworking or baseball cards or anything that you are interested in and as a result, your kids are interested in those things, too. So just imagine what might happen in our churches if from the time our kids were in the nursery to the time they graduated from high school, they grew up regularly hearing from nursery workers, Sunday school teachers, Vacation Bible School staff, youth workers, deacons, and pastors what a joy and privilege it is to serve God in full-time, vocational, career, or lifetime ministry. Just dream with me about what could happen if parents talked regularly to their children about how exciting it would be if God would one day lead them to pursue a career in ministry.

Dream with me about what could happen if parents talked regularly to their children about how exciting it would be if God would one day lead them to pursue a career in ministry.

What if our kids grew up not only hearing or reading about being a doctor, nurse, fireman, policeman, teacher, or lawyer, but also about being a pastor, missionary, youth pastor, curriculum writer or editor, missionary doctor or nurse, camp director, or music and worship leader? What if they grew up wanting to be the next Hudson Taylor, George Mueller, Elizabeth Elliott, Jack Wyrtzen, Ruth Bell Graham, Dwight Moody, or Henrietta Mears. What if they dreamed about doing the kinds of amazing things for God that Moses, Joshua, Hannah, Esther, David, Ruth, Daniel, or Mary did?

I know, I know, you're thinking, "Is this guy serious?" Wrong question! The question ought to be, "What if we took God's Word seriously enough to believe that when Jesus said that the harvest is great but the workers are few and that we should ask God to send workers into the harvest, that He really meant it?"

Some in the church today might answer, "But we shouldn't push our kids to do anything they don't want to do." And I would respond, "Amen!" I find it interesting however, that when these same kids get into high school and Mom and Dad discover that their kids are gifted and skilled enough to get a big scholarship to a big-time university, they don't hesitate to "push" their kids. They think nothing of "pushing" them to pursue a secular career at a secular college with very little thought or prayer given to the possibility that God may have gifted them for lifetime ministry.

Why is it that we assume that students with a 4.0 GPA and a high SAT or ACT score are only "cut out" to be doctors or lawyers rather than pastors or missionaries? Why is it that because a student is a gifted musician that he or she ought to pursue a secular music career? Why is it that a Division I athlete must accept the full-ride scholarship to pursue athletics rather than ministry? Why is it that the brightest and best of our high school graduates are not typically encouraged to think about lifetime ministry? Why does it seem that ministry preparation is only considered if all other career options are closed?

The answer to all of the above questions is fairly simple and straightforward; it is because our eyes are not open. I would like to suggest that there is an eye-opening, thought-changing, biblical principle that must be part of our strategy. God calls it the "Principle of Ownership" and it goes like this, "Do you not know that your body is a temple of the Holy Spirit, who is in you, whom you have received from God? You are not your own; you were bought at a price. Therefore honor God with your body" (1 Corinthians 6:19-20). You need to check out the context, but the short of it is that whether we are running away from sin or pursuing righteousness, the choices we make with our body—what we do, where we go, how we live—need to reflect God's ownership of our life. Jesus Christ bought and paid for us when He died on the cross to pay the penalty for our sin. He paid the debt we owed to God because of our sin and made us the dwelling place for the Holy Spirit. Because He bought and paid for our life, because He lives in us, everything we do and every decision we make must acknowledge His right to do with us as He pleases.

So what's the bottom line? I am convinced that every believer, no matter how intelligent, musical, athletic, dramatic, personable, attractive, gifted, rich or poor he or she may be, ought to consider lifetime ministry as a possibility before looking at any other career choice! If after prayerful consideration and godly counsel, you conclude that God hasn't called you or gifted you for ministry, then pursue what He has called and gifted you to do. In other words, ministry must be your first option, not your last resort!

Ministry must be your first option, not your last resort!

Parents must be helped to realize that this *Principle of Ownership* refers to God's ownership of their son or daughter, not their ownership. As parents, they are stewards of an amazing gift that we call children. Parents are responsible to help those "gifts" determine God's will and direction for their lives. During my years in admissions at Baptist Bible College, I have talked with many students who believed God was leading them to BBC, but were not allowed to come because their parents wanted them closer to home or didn't want them pursuing a career in ministry! That type of thinking is diametrically opposed to God's *Principle of Ownership* and scares the daylights out of me for those parents. One day, they will give an account to God for how they have managed their sons and daughters. I sometimes wonder what those parents will say to God.

By the grace of God, my wife, Jane, and I have watched all three of our children move away from home to pursue God's will for their lives either in the choice of a college or a ministry opportunity. Those are the times when moms cry. They were also the times when this dad cried. Not one of those experiences was easy to handle. We love our kids and it was difficult to let them go, even when we knew they were pursuing God's direction. But that is what we raised our kids to do and we would have been foolish to get in the way.

Besides helping students and parents change their thinking and open their eyes by understanding the *Principle of Ownership*, it is also crucial that the pastor develops a strategy to keep the words of Jesus in Matthew 9 and John 4 before the church on a consistent basis. In planning the preaching calendar for the year, I am not suggesting that both of these texts must be preached each year, although it sure wouldn't hurt. The challenge of "the harvest is great and the workers are few" should be woven into the fabric of as many sermon series as possible in a natural and unforced way.

For example, some churches only preach on giving when the offerings are behind or just before beginning a building program. That's not necessarily wrong, but it would be far more effective if it was done consistently throughout the year so that giving is not perceived as simply a seasonal activity. In the same way, if the challenge to give your life for career ministry only happens during the annual Missions Conference, it only adds to the perception that lifetime ministry is hard, involves a huge amount of financial sacrifice, and usually results in doing something that no one would normally want to do.

God's call to ministry should be an exciting, normal, and natural outcome of years of consistent and intentional teaching and preaching in every ministry of the local church. Just as something is wrong in our churches if we aren't regularly seeing people getting saved and baptized, so too something is wrong when students and adults are not regularly responding to God's direction to lifetime ministry. In fact, we should be disappointed if God isn't sending workers into the harvest in answer to our prayers!

A few years ago, I had the opportunity to meet with five groups of pastors from different areas of the country to challenge them about what they could do to help recruit workers for the harvest. During the meetings, I would ask, "How many of you are in ministry today because someone came alongside of you, told you that they saw great ministry potential in your life, and challenged you to pray about preparing for full-time, career ministry?" In each location, almost every pastor raised his hand. Then I asked, "How many of you are doing the same thing with someone in your church today?" The response was also consistent in each location . . . hardly anyone raised his hand!

I would be negligent if I didn't address the significant cost of preparing for lifetime ministry at a Bible or Christian liberal arts college. I have been involved in Christian higher education for the last eighteen years. I understand the cost of a Christian college education and I understand why students and parents may choose to attend a state or community college. However, I must add that I don't support that choice if it means turning away from God's call to lifetime ministry.

If the local church is going to get serious about sending workers into the harvest field, it must also get serious about providing significant financial support for training and preparing those workers. At a time when many churches, camps, mission agencies, and Christian schools and colleges are struggling to continue the ministries that God has given them, there are no easy answers.

If God tells us to pray for workers for the harvest, God's answer must also include the finances necessary to train and send them into the harvest. I am convinced that our churches must begin to budget significantly for the

Churches must begin to budget significantly for the education and preparation of these students or workers who come from within our own churches.

education and preparation of these students or workers who come from within our own churches. It may be that we don't support as many missionaries and view our students preparing for ministry as future missionaries and pastors. There will always be tension in supporting students preparing for ministry as opposed to students just going to a Christian college. But I am convinced that if the "table has been set" and God has opened the eyes of the people in our churches about raising workers for the harvest, that tension will be greatly decreased or non-existent.

There must also be a balance between supporting students or workers and the colleges who will educate and equip them for ministry. When churches struggle financially, one of the first budget cuts are the Christian colleges. It seems short-sighted, not "open-eyed" to cut those colleges from the budget who are committed to recruiting and preparing lifetime ministers. I recognize that there are no simple solutions to the finances necessary to educate and send workers into the harvest. But I know that the church must get financially involved to a far greater degree than ever before!

Pastors, youth pastors, youth workers, Sunday school teachers, children's ministry leaders, deacons, elders, parents, janitors, ushers, secretaries, interns, and anyone else who regularly walks through the hallways of our churches ought to be praying daily that God would send out workers into the harvest. Pastors and youth pastors must also take the lead in looking for students who have what it takes for ministry and be ready to "come alongside" them to encourage, not pressure, them to pray about pursuing lifetime ministry.

Our churches and homes must be like "greenhouses" that provide an environment that is conducive to spiritual growth and one that will produce the fruit of students who willingly and naturally respond to the need for workers to go out into the harvest. This is what Moses is talking about when he challenged the nation of Israel with these thoughts: "These commandments that I give you today are to be upon your hearts. Impress them on your children. Talk about them when you sit at home and when you walk along the road, when you lie down and when you get up. Tie them as symbols on your hands and bind them on your foreheads. Write them on the doorframes of your houses and on your gates" (Deuteronomy 6:6-9 NIV).

That's it! That is our strategy in a nutshell! Open your eyes, change your thinking, and ask God to send workers into the harvest from your church. Present lifetime ministry as the natural result of knowing our God. Don't focus on what you haven't done in the past. Start challenging your students today with ministry as the greatest and most exciting thing they could ever do with their lives!

REVIEW QUESTIONS

1. List two ways you are encouraging your students to engage in lifetime ministry.

2. Jesus said that we should pray for workers. What could you do to obey this mandate?

3. How can you convey to your students that "doing God's will" can be more satisfying than eating physical food?

4. Set a time to meet with parents to join hands with them in encouraging teens to consider lifetime ministry.

5. Are your students more aware of your patronage to a sports team than they are your passion for lifetime ministry? If so, what are you going to do to change this?

6. What books can you make available to your students to encourage lifetime ministry?

CHAPTER 15

Out of Sight...On Target:
Transitioning Students Beyond Youth Ministry

It was the first Sunday in September and our classroom seemed somewhat empty that day without the presence of last year's seniors. Obviously, we knew they were leaving. Our team of youth workers went to graduation ceremonies in June, and several people from the church went to the seniors' open-house celebrations. It was fun and quite nostalgic to look at the old photographs their parents had displayed. Many of them had attended our church since they were little children. Sure, we knew the seniors were leaving our group at some point, but this was the first week they didn't come to our senior high Sunday school class—and we missed them.

Our team of adult youth workers reminisced a little bit about each of these students and talked about what they had contributed to our youth program. Let me tell you about a few of last year's seniors. Stacy came to everything we did and always sat in the front. She contributed to every discussion, called visitors, and demonstrated solid leadership skills throughout our ministry. She had left early the week before to attend a well-known Christian college.

Josh attended Sunday school almost every week, but missed several weeks of our mid-week youth group meetings each year due to his involvement with the school's cross-country and track teams. He is attending a local community college, but we were not sure where, or if, he went to Sunday school or church services that week.

Emily grew up in our church along with her two older sisters. None of us could recall where any of them went to church when they graduated from high school. In fact, it was sad to realize that we would probably never see her again either.

I could go on with this story, but the reality is that the number one time for people to drop out of church is immediately following high school graduation. The statistics are alarming. Most students who were very active in church and youth group during high school often quit going to church once they enter college.

CURRENT TRENDS

Our graduating seniors are leaving the church! A recent study from Ed Stetzer of LifeWay Research made the national news in publications such as USAToday,[1] revealing the discouraging facts. "Eighty-eight percent of evangelical children are leaving the church shortly after they graduate from high school."[2]

Of course, the same basic trend has been reported by several sources from various denominational backgrounds over the past several months. Take a look at an overview of what is being said by various researchers about this disturbing trend:

* "Two-thirds of all teenagers are unlikely to attend a Christian church after they graduate from high school." - George Barna [3]

* "More than two-thirds of young churchgoing adults in America drop out of church between the ages of eighteen and twenty-two. Most of the dropouts leave the church between the ages of seventeen and nineteen." - Thom Rainer & Sam Rainer III. [4]

* "Seven in 10 Protestants ages 18 to 30 — both evangelical and mainline — who went to church regularly in high school said they quit attending by age 23." - LifeWay Research as reported in USA Today [5]

* "A majority of twentysomethings – 61% of today's young adults – had been churched at one point during their teen years but are now spiritually disengaged." - Barna Research Group [6]

* "Between 30% and 51% of Christians renounce their faith before graduating from college." – *Truth&Conquences* [7]

There is a missing age group in too many of our churches. Students who were once very active in all that the church offered through its youth ministry are so often leaving church once they graduate from high school. We'll explore some of the reasons our students cite for walking away from church later on, but well-known youth ministry educator, Dr. Chap Clark, said at the Vision for Youth Conference, "In most churches, when adolescents leave high school, there are few programmatic options available for them, much less a welcoming community that has committed to bring them into the life of the body." [8]

"In most churches, when adolescents leave high school, there are few programmatic options available for them, much less a welcoming community...."

The solution to this situation is more complex than just offering a program or two for college-age young people, but I agree that far too many churches are not intentional about helping graduating high school students transition into the over-all life of the church. In fact, my observation has been that traditional youth ministry often separates teenagers from other age groups in the church until they leave high school when we kick them out of youth group to forge their own way (spiritually speaking) through their college education, the work force, military service, or other adult responsibilities.

In a recent interview Don Neff said, "Either a church will make intentional connections with the next generation, or it will become a one-generation church and slowly decline." That same sentiment was expressed by Gordon MacDonald in his book *Who Stole My*

"Either a church will make intentional connections with the next generation, or it will become a one-generation church and slowly decline."

Church? "Any church that has not turned its face toward the younger generation will simply cease to exist... We're not talking decades – we're talking just a few years." [9]

WHY ARE THEY LEAVING?

I have spent a great deal of time the last couple of years exploring the causes and solutions for this crisis. My research, reading, experience, and conversations with students, youth workers, parents, and pastors has revealed five significant causes for this exodus from church.

1. **Traditional youth ministry is often characterized by separating generational age groups.**

   I have been in so many churches where the youth room is literally as far away as possible from where the adults meet. It's almost as if churches don't want the two age groups to mingle at all. In fact, I recently visited one of the largest churches in America that was in the process of building an absolutely incredible building exclusively for the church's ministry to teenagers. This edifice contained a huge gym, a concert hall, a coffee house, several offices, and meeting rooms; but they built it on the church property as far away as possible from the main auditorium of the church. This practice seems to be the norm, instead of the exception. Churches tend to isolate the generations along peer lines and the result is often a lack of real, meaningful relationships between teenagers and most adults. It's therefore no wonder when we dismiss them from youth group following high school that they fail to make a positive transition into the adult ministries of the church. Their high school world featured a different program, often a different philosophy of ministry, a different meeting location, different pastors, different musical styles, and very few positive relationships with godly adults. No wonder they walk away.

2. Many youth ministries fail to build loyalty and ownership to the overall church.

Youth workers, you'll have to evaluate your own ministry on this

Are your students more loyal to the youth group than they are to the church as a whole?

one. Are your students more loyal to the youth group than they are to the church as a whole?

Author Robert Laurent made this observation, "In my study, the lack of opportunity for church involvement proved to be the number one reason teens eventually reject religion." [10] That same idea is illustrated by Steve Wright in his book *Rethink*, "It seems that churches of all denominations and sizes are failing to reach teens with the Gospel and baptize them... If our programs are bigger, our budgets are bigger, our shows are bigger, and our workloads as pastors are bigger, then why are baptisms still declining?" [11]

In other words, we must be intentional about helping our students develop a loyalty and ownership of *their* church. The following experience from my own youth ministry provides a tangible illustration of how I learned the importance of this principle. During my early days as a youth pastor, our church hosted a gym night for our teenagers to play pick-up basketball and volleyball. During the evening, one of the older gentlemen in our church came into our gym and with his head down walked through our group and down the stairs at the end of that building. In just a couple of moments all of the lights in the gym went out. This dear saint had flipped the electrical circuit breaker.

He came back up the steps and was making his way across the gym floor when I stopped him by saying, "Sir, what happened?" He responded curtly, "I turned off the lights." Curiously, I asked, "How come?" This was his rationale: "The teenagers don't tithe, so they don't deserve to use church electricity." Then he abruptly walked out. We got those gym lights back on that evening, but his somewhat misguided logic helped me re-evaluate our youth ministry. I determined to help the adults see the benefits of investing in the youth and to help the youth to understand the importance of supporting the church and being loyal.

That conversation helped me see the great value of building loyalty to the church as a whole within the fabric of student ministry. We began to encourage our students to tithe, to get baptized, and to serve within the parameters of the entire church. We taught our young people to participate in church work days, to attend church business meetings, to serve in various church ministries, and to get involved alongside godly adults in appropriate avenues of service with children and adults. The man may have been wrong in what he did but it brought about a good ending.

3. There may be a lack of clear biblical and theological teaching in many of today's student ministries.

Have you ever heard youth workers or other church leaders say something like this: "My teenagers know the Bible. They've heard it all their lives. They need to apply and live what they already know"? I urge you to check it out in your group. I recently visited a church where the youth pastor made this claim when I talked with him about the value of materials and curricula. "My students know the Bible," he boasted, "It's a matter of them learning how to live it out." While I absolutely agree with my friend's last statement, I challenged him on the first part of what he said.

He gave me the opportunity following that morning's church service to meet with a select group of his key students to discern their level of Bible knowledge. I have to admit that this group of students had a basic knowledge of Bible-based facts (for instance, they knew the books of the Bible, they knew about several Bible characters, and they knew some of the general themes of key Bible books). However, they struggled even with a simple understanding of doctrine and theology. Although some of them had strong opinions about some of the basic Bible doctrines, they really struggled knowing how to back up what they believed with Scriptural truth.

Youth workers, we must not ignore the importance of teaching the Bible to our students. My experience tells me that this is a generation that wants to know what they believe and why. (I highly recommend that every youth worker and church leader read and devour Dr. Christian Smith's classic report on the Millennial Generation's religious faith: *Soul Searching: The Religious and Spiritual Lives of American Teenagers*. Some of his findings will challenge your thinking and some will almost break your heart.)

4. **Many churches are weak in developing spiritual leadership in the lives of maturing teenagers.**

I am afraid that we have been acting as if our teenagers are little kids. So, we try to entertain them and spoon feed them instead of asking them for a growing commitment toward what it really means to follow Christ. I believe that the very nature of youth ministry provides an obvious visual aid of what this idea could look like. I'll phrase it in the form of a question. Do you treat your seniors in high school the same way you treat the freshmen? Doesn't it make sense to think that many of our upper classmen should be more mature in Christ and farther along in their spiritual development than they were as ninth graders?

We'll talk more about this point below when we get to the solutions, but suffice it to say that our student ministries should be places of spiritual growth and maturity that produce high school seniors, then young adults, and ultimately fully-functioning and church-active adults who demonstrate a growing commitment to Christ and His church and who live out a maturing influence on others.

5. **Too many churches do not intentionally help students transition from youth group into the overall life of the church.**

My last observation about why this departure happens is that we are quite weak at helping teenagers transition from their culture of adolescence into a world of commitment and responsibility of adulthood. I think Chap Clark (quoted above) got it right when he talks about the "few programmatic options" available in many, many churches following high school ministry. Not only should churches make ministries for young adults a key ingredient of their overall educational plan, they should also intentionally build sensitivity toward all generations into the framework of their worship and fellowship experiences and programs.

I appreciate the intergenerational emphasis in Gary MacIntosh's book *One Church; Four Generations*: "It is crucial that the worship team be intergenerational. The leaders who are seen on the platform influence the people who will attend the service. When people come to a church, one of the first things they do is look around to find people like themselves."[12] He makes a good point. Our churches must be God-honoring places where children, young people, young adults, and older adults alike serve Him and worship Him. It is a shame if churches are humanly willing to overlook or exclude any particular age group.

There are several practical ways churches can bridge the generation gap that exists in so many churches between teenagers and adults. First of all, I am a huge fan of building intentional mentoring connections in the church where caring and Godly adults seek to develop growing relationships with individual young people. [13] I advocate that this can operate beyond the structure of a typical youth ministry that features a small team of adults who serve as "official" youth workers. Churches can recruit a larger group of caring adults to serve as spiritual mentors for the teenagers. These adults can form positive relationships with kids that will carry over from youth ministry into adult ministry with this by-product: kids will get to know some of the adults on a personal level.

Another way I've seen churches help graduating high school seniors make this transition is through an intergenerational approach to small groups. If your church is working on a small group ministry, why not consider making each of the groups intergenerational in nature? I have seen this to be a very positive thing for churches when young adults and older adults meet together in small group settings for Bible study, prayer, and fellowship.

SOME POSSIBLE SOLUTIONS

Youth workers, we all must do a better job helping our students transition out of youth group and into the adult ministries of our churches—or help to get them actively plugged into a church in the community where they go to college! Our main objective must not be to get them to high school graduation and out of our programs. Instead it must be for them to go on for God for the remainder of their adult lives.

> *Our main objective must not be to get them to high school graduation and out of our programs.*

This single chapter does not do justice to this critical topic, but here are a few suggestions to consider as you face the issue of your high school graduates walking away from church once they leave your youth ministry.

1. **Equip parents to see the importance of regular church involvement for their children in high school and in college.**

   The real issue here, of course, is that if parents see church attendance and church involvement as critically important in their own lives, their children will be more likely to grow up with those same values. However, if parents of teenagers allow work, school, athletic involvement, or other things to come before church, the students will probably grow up with the idea that church is somewhere down the line on the priority list. This doesn't mean that we should be legalistic about not missing even one week of church. Many kids today are busy and I've met several students all across the country who have the ability to juggle the demands of teenage life with a high commitment to Jesus Christ and His church. This just means that we must help our people make a commitment to church involvement because they see it is important to God.

   Personally, my parents didn't give me a choice in this. No matter what, church was first. Not the high school basketball team, not a job, not homework—nothing came before our family's commitment to our church. That value stayed with me into college and on into adult life. I don't think it's naïve to believe that emphasis will work today as well. That's why I tell youth workers to equip the parents of teenagers in their youth groups to make church involvement a top priority in the lives of their children now.

A few weeks ago I met a set of parents who had just dropped off their daughter for an early-admit program at a state university a few hours drive from their home. These parents, after hearing me speak about the solutions to the above-quoted statistics about our kids leaving the church, admitted that while they were at the university, they were involved in paying their child's school bill, moving their daughter into her dorm room, helping her select her classes, and even making sure that she had a parking place on campus, but they never took the time to see if there was a good church in that community. Church involvement is a family issue first, and all youth workers should do their best to help parents see the importance of consistent involvement in God's church.

2. Build leadership skills into the lives of your students as they progress throughout their senior high years.

Youth group must be more than entertainment and a place to hang out with friends. It must be a place of intentional transition from spiritual childhood into God-honoring adult maturity. Simply put, youth group must be a place where high school seniors have more leadership responsibility than ninth graders do. If we want our kids to stay in church after high school, it is very important that we give them increasing levels of leadership involvement as they progress throughout our ministries. Developing student leadership may be more important than we ever realized.

> *Youth group must be a place of intentional transition from spiritual childhood into God-honoring adult maturity.*

There's another perspective to this matter that I want to share with readers. I have personally talked to several youth workers who told me that they have many high school seniors who virtually "check out" of youth group long before they graduate from high school. These students were very active as freshman or sophomores, but became less and less involved as they progressed through high school. Is that happening in your group? Perhaps it is because our youth programs are exactly the same year after year. In some churches, the basic structure of youth ministry is the same for seniors as it is for seventh graders. No wonder kids get bored and quit coming! That's why it is so critical to develop student leadership as students grow throughout our youth ministries. (By the way, I present some specific ideas on this issue in my book *Impacting the Next Generation: A Strategy for Discipleship in Youth Ministry*, available at http://www.rbpstore. org/productView/showprod.cfm?prodnum=5288.)

The solution, of course, is to give your high school seniors more and more leadership responsibilities in youth group and in church as they mature. You'll want to make sure that these students are actively living for the Lord so that a lifestyle of carnality and sin is not promoted. However, I really believe that students are much more likely to stay involved in church throughout their college-age years and into their adult lives if they are encouraged to develop specific leadership skills as they progress through their years in your youth ministry. Specifically, I'm talking about giving your older kids opportunities to mentor the younger kids in the group and to be involved in other key avenues of hands-on ministry as juniors and seniors. If churches are going to be proactive about keeping their teenagers in church after they graduate, then it's time to be serious about developing leadership in the lives of maturing students.

3. Develop a genuine loyalty to the whole church, not just the youth group.

As I said above, I'm afraid that in typical youth ministries, kids are more loyal to the youth group than they are to the church as a whole. If this is the case, it's no wonder that they don't want to be a part of the church itself after they leave youth group. They graduate from high school, we make them leave youth group, and then they struggle to find their place in the larger church community. They don't seem to fit into the adult world of the church, so they tend to feel like the proverbial fish-out-of-water, missing the familiar safety and security of the youth group. Wise youth workers will deliberately ensure that teenagers realize they are a part of the local church as a whole instead of isolating students in the cocoon of the youth group. Ways to do this include providing kids with opportunities for significant ministry, teaching them to give financially (including the discipline of tithing), and giving them positive interaction with people from other age groups. I also recommend that (if at all possible) the church's senior pastor be actively involved in the lives of teenagers. He is their pastor, too. Students need to grow up realizing that they are a part of something bigger than their own world of peers.

4. **Carefully teach your students the Word of God, including the ability to personalize doctrinal truth.**

Contemporary sociologists and church leaders alike are realizing that college-age young adults are struggling to know what they believe. This is the age when students must come to terms with the importance of clear-cut, rock-solid doctrinal truth. This generation wants to know what they believe. It doesn't matter if they go to a Bible college, a major state university, or enter the military or workforce, these young adults will be forced to evaluate their own personal belief system. They'll ask themselves, time and time again, "Do I really believe this?"

That's why it is so important for our teaching ministries to be much, much more than just quick devotionals we get ready at the last minute. So many youth workers build their teaching times around hot topics of the day or teen-generated subjects instead of the "whole counsel of God" that includes solid Bible content and in-depth doctrinal truth. If we look at youth ministry as a terminal program (i.e., it has a clear beginning and ending), we'll realize that we have a very short amount of time to make sure that our kids are prepared to face an adult world knowing what they believe based on the complete, inerrant, and inspired Word of God.

5. Be intentional about developing wholesome connections between adults and teenagers in your church.

My last suggestion for youth workers on this subject is something I alluded to earlier in this chapter: the importance of building strong intergenerational connections into the lives of students. We are making a mistake if we isolate teenagers into their own little sub-culture of youth ministry. However, isolation seems to be the prevalent practice of so many of today's youth ministries. Adolescents need and desire healthy and growing relationships with godly adults. This seems to be the pattern espoused in Titus 2, for instance, as Paul instructed Titus to develop strategic intergenerational ministries in the early church.

Let me be clear, I am not advocating a total departure from peer ministry. I believe in youth ministry, and I can argue for the value of a strong, vibrant church youth program. However, teens need adults and vice versa. The generations will often become very absorbed into their own cultural worlds of friends and experiences if they are not making intentional intergenerational relationships. The research is clear. We must break down generational barriers that tend to develop selfishness around externals such as music, fashion, and other cultural trends.

We must break down generational barriers that tend to develop selfishness around externals

CONCLUSION

I wouldn't mind that empty classroom I spoke about in the beginning of this chapter if our team of youth workers knew that Stacy, Josh, and Emily were heartily welcomed into a caring community of believers in an active adult or young adult Bible fellowship or Sunday school class that demonstrated genuine love and a heart for ministry to and with them. That may be the key to the situation I am describing here— godly adults who are totally committed to welcoming members of a new generation into the overall life of the church. After all, there is really no such thing as graduating from church!

REVIEW QUESTIONS

1. Make a list of the graduating seniors from your youth group last year. Where are they now? Are they active in church anywhere? Why or why not?

2. Take a quick overview of your church: what organized ministries are one-generational (people of similar age groups meeting together); what ministries are multi-generational (people of various age groups attending the same functions but rarely interacting with each other); and what ministries are truly inter-generational (where the generations meet together with mutual interaction and fellowship)?

3. Does your church have an intentional plan to help graduating seniors transition into the life of adult ministries in your church?

4. What practical ways could you suggest to develop healthy and growing intergenerational relationships in your church?

5. Take a quick assessment of all age groups in your church. Do they know what they believe theologically? How are your church educational ministries helping your people know what they believe based upon Scriptural truth?

CHAPTER 16

So Now What?
Creating Students of Influence

In the days leading up to the Civil War, Ralph Waldo Emerson has been credited as saying, "We are living in anxious times." We are still living in anxious times. The twenty-first century, it seems, is just as divided and selfish as our ancestors'. What is God's antidote for today? It is the same as it was in the mid-1800's. I submit to you that although methods may change, God's plan is still the same.

It is the exact same plan He used when He created a nation out of that which would come: a people, a book, and a Savior. It was the same when He wanted to lead His people out of Egypt, or lead a queen who would plead for her people, or lead a shepherd boy to slay a giant, or call a Pharisee to carry the message of Jesus Christ to the world. His prescribed cure and assigned plan has never wavered. His plan is to call out leaders from people just like you and me so He can energize them to accomplish extraordinary, world-changing activities.

Scripture is so clear that God is searching for men and women who will first answer His call and then stand strong.

Scripture is so clear that God is searching for men and women who will first answer His call and then stand strong: "So I sought for a man among them who would make a wall and stand in the gap before Me on behalf of the land" (Ezekiel 22:30). Wow! What a perfect description of leadership as influence. This simple verse not only applies to past leaders God used but it also describes how a young man or woman can be used today. Remember, the Lord still uses an individual, not a committee. He has always chosen, "One from among them," one who will connect with their culture and influence their community, one who will build a wall.

The good news is that even though it appears the world is in a mess and the local church is far from what the Lord intended, the Lord Himself modeled for us that you can take your twelve or twenty or seventy influencers and "turn the world right side up." There is power in the fellowship of a committed few. That is why I started Student Leadership University (SLU). After traveling the world to speak with students, I sat down with fifty student pastors and simply asked, "If you could do this all over again, what would you do differently?" The answer was overwhelmingly simple: "I would spend more time equipping my core group of student leaders."

But that same group of student pastors was struggling with an increasingly smaller summer window of ministry and an increasingly busier student population. The challenge they placed before me was, "Give us a turnkey package that will give our students a quantum leap in the rules and tools of leadership, and make it different from youth camp or a missions trip."

At SLU, students experience hands-on interactive leadership training with an uniquely biblical perspective. They are challenged to think and act as leaders. More than thirty thousand students have now experienced this amazing program. Every year I receive stories of how alumni are making huge impacts in corporate, government, and ministry sectors. This is all taking place because we are committed to creating students of influence. We want young people to understand that they can have God's power and presence today no matter

We want young people to understand that they can have God's power and presence today no matter the size or the difficulty of life.

the size or the difficulty of life.

So what seems to be the hold-up? Let's put first things first and deal with the three critical questions in your journey to influence and leadership:

1. Who are you and what gives you the right to lead others?
2. Who are you attempting to impact? Do you understand the times and have the knowledge of what you should and can do?
3. What does an influencer look like?

QUESTION №1 – WHO ARE YOU AND WHAT GIVES YOU THE RIGHT TO LEAD OTHERS?

It is not merely being elected to a position or being given a title or even earning a degree that qualifies or gives us that right. In fact, the right to lead and influence must be earned. My good friend, Dr. John Maxwell, says it best, "The key is becoming the kind of person that people willingly want to follow."

Therefore you and I must commit ourselves to becoming the person who can take them where they need to go. Students need to be introduced to the truth that they must first "BE" before they can ever "DO." If we are to assist student leaders in leaving a lasting, eternal imprint on this generation through their influence, then we must deal with core issues.

But *influence* doesn't come easy; influence always requires courage.

Influence doesn't come easy; influence always requires courage.

You must put your heart, your all, on the line. Jackie Robinson, the legendary baseball player once said, "A life isn't significant except for its impact on others' lives." It's no wonder that he was so greatly used to help crash the gate in race relations for professional sports. Too often we want the big event, the quick fix to do all the heavy lifting for us. But I assure you, the lesson of raising a generation to influence the world won't be learned in the middle of a pep rally or a conference. These levels of impact can only take place one student at a time.

You are reading this book in order to be able to "Push the Limits" in your student ministry and to prepare yourself to become a better leader. Use these guidelines to grow yourself. You will be better prepared if you allow those characteristics to fill your life.

QUESTION №2 – WHO ARE YOU ATTEMPTING TO IMPACT? DO YOU UNDERSTAND THE TIMES AND HAVE KNOWLEDGE OF WHAT YOU SHOULD AND CAN DO?

Recently I was privileged to speak at the National Religious Broadcasters convention on the subject of reaching the next generation. In my research on the millennial generation, I was reminded of a phrase I coined a few years back: "Tradigital Strategies for Reaching and Keeping Students." I am certain that today, more than ever, we need to deliver the traditional values and traditional foundations of the faith, but we must do so with a new digital platform. Thus, I want to share with you part of the profile that I gave those in attendance at the National Religious Broadcasters Convention.

Reaching and Keeping the Millennial Generation

The millennial generation, those born between the years 1979 through 1999, is a huge generation of impatient, experiential learners, digital natives, multi-taskers, and gamers who love the flat, networked world and expect nomadic connectivity 24/7. They are demanding consumers who expect more selectivity, personalization, and customization in their products and services. This is a generation that has never known a world without wireless connectivity or a world without limitless digital resources.

They are the second largest generation in U.S. history, barely smaller than the baby boomers. This generation is consuming media at an unprecedented rate. Unlimited media is readily available through the internet and portable devices like ipods and cell phones. This generation has an almost insatiable appetite for media in every possible format. They have no brand loyalty but do have great viral capacity. This generation will be the first to literally reach worldwide with the simplistic keystrokes of a laptop while enjoying a latte in their local Starbucks.

They are more likely to consume Christian content in a secular society, as secular platforms tend to lend credibility to a Christian message in this new digital world. Millennials expect a much greater array of product and service selectivity. They have grown up with a huge array of choices and they believe that such abundance is their birthright. Millennials will choose any or all types of music. No one type of music prevails for the majority. Millennials are the first generation without a unique generational music. Millennials prefer to keep their time and commitments flexible longer in order to take advantage of better options; they also expect other people and institutions to give them more flexibility. Millennials, by their own admission, have no tolerance for delays.

So where does this leave us? In today's real world, *technology is the medium*. The use of entertainment through technology to deliver a powerful, life-changing message has become essential in the race to reach the millennials. The millennial mind requires low effort and high excitement. This amazing generation is open to new and relevant technology and rushes to experience new technology like no other generation, but this generation is also more aware of quality and relevance like no other generation.

For example, podcasts and video downloads have rapidly replaced traditional television as the preferred delivery of content. Movies remain a medium of delivery that attracts this generation of experiential consumers. There have been some incredible crossover deliverables into this generation that we can learn from:

Facing the Giants: (www.facingthegiants.com) This movie, which has had phenomenal success in the box office, is an example of how a local church in Albany, Georgia embraced a secular delivery model (the movie theatre) and will be impacting teams, students, business leaders, and ministries for years to come, all because they understood how to deliver a traditional message to a digital generation through a secular platform. Remember, this generation knows quality immediately and will embrace the message more readily in a secular environment, like a movie theatre where they also saw a blockbuster feature the weekend before. Facing the Giants has a strategy that you can embrace, allowing you to engage your community with this full-featured production as a tool to reach your school, team, or community.

FXL: (www.lightstogether.com) This amazing technology combines the best of Facebook, My Space, and iTunes all in one open platform. With the multi-tasking capacity of the millennial, this open-platform Christian community is setting the standard for digital communities of the future.

GodTube: (www.tangle.com) YouTube turned the Internet world upside down and now GodTube (now known as *Tangle*) has the capacity to turn the world right side up through a full-featured, user-friendly platform for this generation to openly share Christian content in a safe environment with the quality they have already experienced through YouTube.

The Word of Promise: (www.thewordofpromise.com) This "audio theater" of the Bible is a very good example of what this generation will gravitate toward. It involves household Hollywood stars like Jim Caviezel, Marissa Tomei, and others in a world-class production that will allow the Word of God to come alive through superb media delivery. This Thomas Nelson product is available in your local bookstore.

Walking the Bible: (www.walkingthebible.com) This has become one of Public Broadcasting's most watched TV series. This all-high definition production utilizes new video technologies to allow the realities of archeology and history to tell the story of the Old Testament. Production on three new biblical series has already been approved to tell the story of the Gospels, of the history of Christianity, and the history of the city of Jerusalem. Through internet, television, and the big and tiny screen, *Walking the Bible* is another example of a Tradigital tool that has lasting impact.

We live in an "experience" economy today. Learning now requires experience which leads to action. We should utilize multiple arenas to make leadership come alive. What about learning how to deal with difficult people while you are in the shark tank inside Sea World? Or how about experiencing the price of freedom by visiting the beaches of Normandy? The ultimate outcome is that we are intrigued, educated, and then engaged in actions that are changing the world. By the way, these are true scenarios students experience at SLU.

QUESTION №3 - WHAT DOES AN INFLUENCER LOOK LIKE?

Webster's dictionary defines *influence* as:

> The act or power of producing an effect without apparent exertion of force or direct exercise of command.

> The power or capacity of causing an effect in indirect or intangible ways.

Intentional

Nurturer

Focused

Leadership

Universal Outlook

Enthusiasm

Nevertheless

Credibility

Evangelism

Let's turn the puzzle box cover over. Scripture is overflowing with examples and profiles of both positive and negative influencers. Let's model the following character traits and skills that they made by consistently displaying integrity. I am convinced that students will understand and live a life of integrity but integrity is caught more than taught. Influence and leadership must be lived, not read about or discussed. It must be lived out in a life of intentional activity.

Influence and leadership must be lived, not read about or discussed.

What is often overlooked is this fact: "Everything rises and falls on leadership." The single greatest one-word definition of leadership is *influence*. One of my all-time favorite teachers, Dr. Howard Hendricks, who has trained thousands of youth pastors around the world, observed, "You can inform from a distance, you can entertain from a distance, but you can only influence and impact by being up close and personal." If it's my passion to be an influencer, I must possess the following skills and character traits. By using the acrostic INFLUENCE, let's look at nine key elements:

Intentional: I want the students that I'm attempting to disciple and mentor to be fueled with intention. In fact to be perfectly honest, I want you who are desirous of influencing your influencers to be fueled with intention. Being intentional has best been described as "living life on purpose." Intentional living fuels your passion and your purpose. It requires a daily quiet time with God the Father. In order to complete this grueling race called life, you must schedule the necessary pit stops. You cannot allow anything or anyone to rob you of this essential time.

Joe Paterno, the legendary Penn State football coach states, "We need people who influence their peers and who cannot be detoured from their convictions by peers who do not have the courage to have convictions."[1] When put on public display for others to read, what does your life say? Your reputation for intentional living should be talked about in the halls so that others will see it and enthusiastically join you in living for Christ. Living intentionally means you choose carefully your thoughts, your motives, and your actions. Your life is designed by integrity and sincerity.

Nurturer: To be a spiritual leader and to raise up other spiritual leaders, you must first be a spiritual servant. A nurturer is one who constantly and consistently appreciates and esteems. In fact, the Bible teaches in Philippians 2:3, that we must esteem others higher than we do ourselves. It's not that you think less of yourself; it's just that you think about yourself less. Dr. Fred Williams taught me a valuable lesson as a young preacher when he said, "Jay, picture yourself in the balcony pulling people up to where you are with words of encouragement, rather than being a basement person who is holding or pulling people down."

Focused: The Chinese have a wonderful proverb, "If you chase two rabbits, both will escape." Oftentimes I'm afraid that's what happens to those of us in youth ministry. We have so many responsibilities and so many dreams and goals that we seldom accomplish that which is the most important. We know that focus is one of the greatest strengths of an effective leader. The key is to establish your priorities and then to concentrate on those priorities. The ability to harness both of those allows you to move from being merely efficient to being wildly effective.

The key is to establish your priorities and then to concentrate on those priorities.

Joshua and Caleb greatly illustrate the power of focus. They were given the assignment, along with ten others, to go spy out the land of Israel. Unfortunately, the other ten were easily distracted. They began to focus on how big the problems were. You remember the giants, the walled city, the vastness of the land, and so on. My friend,General Schwarzkopf was correct when he said the easiest way to be defeated was to be distracted.

In ministry we often major so much on what we can't do that we fail to focus on what we can. If we overly focus on what we don't have, we usually fail to utilize what we do possess. Far too often we confuse motion with progress. Joshua and Caleb magnified the potential and the promise. You can almost hear Joshua and Caleb shouting to us today, "*The bigger your God, the smaller your obstacles!*" Your focus will keep you fueled and faithful and it will enable you to be a finisher.

Leadership: This is a difficult word to define in the truest sense. In studying the greatest leadership manual I believe ever written, the Bible, I find there are many characteristics that mark a biblical leader. We must instill this into our "twelve" or our "twenty" leaders. A leader is one whose first thought is positive. This is quite refreshing in a very negative world. A biblical leader has a habit of making their first action step a positive step. In other words, a positive thought is not enough. A leader must be willing to take a positive step in the direction of fulfilling that thought. A leader is one who sees the big picture—which is often why we have conflicts on our church staff. Unfortunately, some of us who work with students are seen as not caring about the budget or the children's ministry or the music ministry and so forth. Therefore seeing the big picture means we're seen as a team player.

One of my very favorite ways to demonstrate servant leadership is the fact that we have so many outstanding college interns from some of America's leading Christian universities who serve middle and high school students at our SLU programs. It's quite impressive watching the president of his student body or one of the most popular athletes or a student ranked among the highest academically caring deeply and working so hard as they serve younger students who will probably never be in a position to do anything for them.

Universal Outlook: Jesus not only taught the Great Commandment but He also gave us the Great Commission to go into the entire world and preach the Gospel to every creature. In Matthew, He commanded us to go into all the nations and make disciples. His last words on the earth, from the Book of Acts, challenged us to begin in Jerusalem, and spread to Judea and the uttermost part of the world. Here in the twenty-first century where you and I have been called to minister, He's brought the whole world to us. In virtually every town, city, and village in America, there are pockets of other nationalities that have moved to America. He brought the whole world to us. If you and I are to influence this generation, we must teach them to see through the lenses of Jesus those who may be different from us in color, clothing, and customs. I believe this generation will definitely respond to a Jesus model of no longer "us versus them" but all of us together for Him. Dr. Bill Bright certainly had a burden for us all when he said, "Believe the best is yet to come and believe the best."

Enthusiasm: As you no doubt know by now, enthusiasm comes from the words *en theos* which means "God in you." Passion is without question the first step to achievement. History is saturated with ordinary people who accomplished extraordinary things but they did so because they had great desire. Your desire will determine your destiny. Exceptional achievements result from internal convictions rather than external circumstances. I believe passion is the result of a mission that motivates. Enthusiasm is the call to action. It

> *Passion is without question the first step to achievement.*

is the ignition that starts the inner engine revving. Rick Warren said it so well when he spoke to those of us in leadership positions: "If we truly want to know the temperature of our church or youth group, we must stick the thermometer in our own mouth." In essence, if we're not refueled and reenergized with the fire of Heaven burning in our hearts, how in the world will our students become passionate, devoted followers of Christ?

Nevertheless: This is perhaps one of my greatest prayers for all of us who want to influence this generation and to ignite a spirit of "nevertheless" in our students. The life of David demonstrated this spirit, the spirit that says, "If God be for me, who can be against me." It was this spirit that propelled him from a mere lad to a leader, from a shepherd boy to a sovereign, from the pasture to the palace. The Bible tells us that David was attacked by a lion but "nevertheless" he killed it. On another occasion while tending his father's flocks, they were attacked by a bear but "nevertheless" he killed it. He grew weary of hearing the taunts and the mocking of the giant. When everyone else in the army of Israel cowered with fear and exclaimed that Goliath was too big to kill, David grew angry that the Lord was being mocked and proved with one small stone that he was too big to miss. "Nevertheless," David killed the giant!

Credibility: Jim Collins, in one of the greatest business books ever written[2], defines *credibility*. People look for four things in those they will *willingly* follow. Please underscore that word. Just because you have the title, job, or position doesn't mean anything to this generation. Most student leaders find themselves on the bottom of a typical organizational chart, but I assure you that your leaders, students, and church know if you are a leader of credibility. It is imperative that we be credible and that we possess these four characteristics, then instill them in our students:

* *Honesty* – Your first word must be your best word. Do people believe what you are saying is true? We must never ever lie or exaggerate. It always undermines our credibility.

* *Forward Thinking* – Once again, vision is the single greatest leadership trait you can possess. We would do our students well to maintain an optimistic faithful view of the future. Corrie Ten

Boom signed all of her letters even in the direst of circumstances with "the best is yet to be."

* *Competence* – Are you good at what you do? It's one reason why we try so hard to help youth workers, whether full-time or volunteer, to organize or agonize. In other words, to learn how to manage themselves, their time, tongue, and the projects put into their hands. Both the adults you must motivate and the students you must lead will want to sense you know what you are doing.

* *Inspiring* – We must be able to communicate our vision and to inspire by our words and our deeds. One thing I never forget is that if I can't motivate myself, I'll never be able to motivate others. Charles Wesley, the most published hymn writer to ever live stated, "I set myself on fire and others came to watch me burn."

Evangelism: This is perhaps that which I believe to be closest to the heart of Jesus. The sharing of the good news of the Gospel is not optional. It is imperative that you have on your calendar three or four intentional and well-planned events for the sole purpose of evangelism. It might be a concert with an invitation at the end. It might be a fifth quarter after a football or basketball game with a dynamic young speaker. It might be gathering a complete list of every student on your role, those who attend and those who have dropped out, so you can connect with them and share your faith. Help your students know how to be a leader on their school campuses for Christ. I often tell students, "If you're not an influencer for the Gospel on your campus, you're really not much of a leader no matter how often you attend church."

As a young man, Abraham Lincoln worried that the "field of glory" had been harvested by the founding fathers and that, nothing had been left for his generation but modest ambitions. In the 1850s, however, the wheel of history turned."[3] The wheel of history will turn for your generation and the generation of your students. This world desperately needs students of influence to seize their chance to influence this planet for Christ. May you be a leader that God uses to influence students so they can reach this generation!

> **The sharing of the good news of the Gospel is not optional.**

REVIEW QUESTIONS

1. What are your responsibilities in student ministry?

2. Who are you really? Do you allow students to see the real you?

3. Why do you want to lead youth?

4. Do you understand the times and have the knowledge of what you should and can do?

5. What does an influencer look like?

6. What two areas of leadership do you need to develop in order to have the greatest impact on students?

APPENDIX A

Moving On - Exercise

Please take this exercise with you to the mission field and complete it during the last week of your mission experience.

Complete the following sentences with your own words. You may write whatever comes to mind. You may want to use another sheet of paper for space to write full answers.

LEAVING

1. When I think of leaving my host country, I feel...

2. My experience here has been...

3. For me   (name of country)   means . . .

4. The people I will miss are...

5. The things that I will miss are...

6. The things I will be happy to leave behind are...

7. When leaving a place I usually...

8. The easiest point of leaving for me will be...

9. Before I leave I really want to...

10. I feel that my goals/expectations have been...

11. The most stressful part of leaving will be...

EXPECTATIONS

12. I expect that the process of returning will be...

13. I expect the reception from my family will be...

14. I expect the reception from my church will be...

15. I expect the reception from my friends will be...

16. I think my church will expect me to...

17. I think my family will expect me to...

18. I think my friends at home will expect me to...

19. If my career does not work out I will...

RETURNING

20. When I think of returning to the U.S., I feel...

21. I will be going back to...

22. Regarding money, I will be...

23. Going back will enable me to...

24. I think the hardest part of going back for me will be...

25. I think the easiest part of going back for me will be...

26. I am really looking forward to...

APPENDIX B

Debriefing
30 Questions to ask

1. What were the high points and the low points?

2. Who most encouraged you on the trip?

3. Did you accomplish your goals?

4. What did God do?

5. What stories can you share?

6. What pictures did you like best?

7. Describe some of the relationships you made.

8. What did you find most challenging?

9. Were you well prepared? What else could you have done?

10. How would you rate the unity in your team?

11. How are you doing physically?

12. How are you doing emotionally?

13. How are you doing spiritually?

14. Did anything disappoint you about yourself?

15. What surprised you about the culture?

16. What ministry skills did you sharpen?

17. Did you find fulfillment in your ministry time?

18. What did you learn about ministry?

19. Did you experience any miracles in your ministry time?

20. What comes next for you in life?

21. What do you hope to accomplish in the next year?

22. What is your plan to get there?

23. What changes do you want to make to your life?

24. Are there any relationships you need to change?

25. How will you change them?

26. What concerns do you have as you go back home?

27. Who can help you keep the flame alive back home?

28. What ministry will you continue to do in the community?

29. What can you do to go to the next level spiritually?

30. Who will you reach out and minister to?

APPENDIX C

Settling Back In - Exercise
(To be completed 1-2 months after returning home)

Complete the following sentences with your own words. You may write whatever comes to mind. You may want to use another sheet of paper for space to write full answers.

1. Now that I am back home, I feel...

2. I find it easy to...

3. I find it hard to...

4. I wish...

5. The people who I feel understand me are...

6. I enjoy being with...

7. I enjoy (activity)...

8. My family says I...

9. My friends say I...

10. My pastor says I...

11. I need help in...

APPENDIX D

Church Summer-Servant Program
For students who have completed grades seven
through twelve.

GOAL: To help students gain first-hand experience in the challenge of church-related ministries. Also, to stimulate spiritual growth through a discipleship type of learning.

HOUSING AND FOOD: At home, except for camps, conference, or occasional weekend ministries.

REQUIREMENTS OF ITS MEMBERS:

1. A nine-week commitment to a wide variety of responsibilities and special activities.

2. A teachable attitude.

3. A desire to grow spiritually.

4. A willingness to make personal sacrifices in order to commit time and work necessary for the success of the program. (Person applying should plan on outside employment.)

5. A personal commitment to the maintenance of a Christian "Life Journal" of summer activities and growth.

6. The agreement of parents to this type of involvement in church ministries.

7. A few financial fees.

SPECIFIC SCHEDULE: Basically the schedule is a half-day of committed time. Exceptions are during weeks of camp, conference, or ministries. There are also necessary, brief Bible study sessions twice a week for Scripture studies, sharing, and Bible memorization.

LEADERSHIP: Summer servants will be given leadership by the church youth pastor, intern or committed adults. Openings are limited to six teens per adult leader.

SPONSORSHIP: Although minimal fees are required of summer servants, the local church will help subsidize camp, conference, and other expenses.

INTERESTED PERSONS: Should apply to their pastor by May 15. They should be willing to write why they want to be a summer servant. They must also state times they would be out of town during the summer since this is an important consideration in acceptance for the program. In addition, both young person and parents must sign the following statement (parents' signature indicates consent and cooperation): "If accepted as a summer servant, I will be consistent and faithful in attending and fulfilling the summer servant activities and responsibilities. I will follow the instructions of the summer servant director. I will be willing to learn new skills and be a servant to God for other people."

IDEAS FOR A SCHEDULE OF SUMMER SERVANTS (done by each church)

1. Weekend (overnight) orientation and training retreat.
2. Help with neighborhood Bible clubs and building relationships with children—puppet, drama, and craft times. (Bring a sack lunch.)
3. Present a children's church program.
4. Plan four youth "get-away days" for any interested students. These include a day-long trip to museums, parks, and so forth for various youth.
5. Serve as helpers for camp.
6. Do painting and yard work around the church.

7. Visit shut-ins, present programs at nursing homes, visit a rescue mission.

8. Publish at least three youth pages for the church bulletin or website.

9. Do puppet spots at hospitals and community locations.

10. Do yard work for needy people.

11. Door-to-door evangelism. Help with VBS promotion.

12. Plan and present one entire mid-week service.

13. Help with VBS—Bible stories, crafts, recreation, decorations.

14. Attend Momentum Conference (week-long youth event).

15. Take a ministry trip to a church to help with their youth work, outreach, or music.

16. Attend all youth meetings at the church.

17. Do required devotional study and memorization for the meeting twice.

18. Write in "Life Journal" daily as a record of Bible studies, messages you heard or gave, impressions, and so forth—a type of scrapbook.

19. Summer servants Recognition and Award Banquet.

WHAT THE STUDENTS CAN EXPECT TO RECEIVE:

1. Training in various church ministries.

2. Discipleship.

3. Assessment of their strengths and weaknesses and how they could best serve the Lord in the future.

4. Financial assistance to attend camps or events during the summer.

5. An opportunity to learn outreach, discipleship, ministry skills, children's ministries, and time management.

6. An opportunity to impact hundreds of people through a local church.

7. Prayer support from the church for each servant as we list students' names in the church bulletin or prayer sheets.

END NOTES

Chapter 1

1. Derek Melleby, "Life after high school: The first year," *CPYU* www.cpyu.org/Page.aspx?id=387650 (25 March 2009).

2. Walt Mueller, "Culture Watch," *Youth Worker Journal,* November/December 2008.

3. Lawrence O. Richards, *Christian Education: Seeking to Become Like Jesus Christ* (Grand Rapids, MI: Zondervan, 1988), 31.

Chapter 2

1. Tim Hansen, *The Market's 10 Best Stocks Revealed,* www.fool. com/investing/small-cap/2008/07/17/the-markets-10-best-stocks-revealed.aspx (2 April 2009).

2. John C. Maxwell, *The 21 Indispensable Qualities of a Leader* (Nashville, TN: Thomas Nelson, 1999), ix.

3. Leroy Eims, *Be the Leader You Were Meant To Be, Growing Into the Leader God Called You* to Be (Colorado Springs, CO: David C. Cook, 1975), 116.

4. John Maxwell, *Developing the Leader Within You* (Nashville, TN: Thomas Nelson, 1993), 38

5. Dr. Waylon Moore, *The Power of a Mentor* (Tampa, FL: Missions Unlimited, 1996), 13

6. Will Allen Dromgoole, in "Wikipedia, The Free Encyclopedia." en.wikipedia.org/wiki/The_Bridge_Builder (27 March, 2009)

Chapter 3

1. Leroy Eims, *The Lost Art of Disciple Making* (Grand Rapids, MI: Zondervan, 1978), 28

Chapter 4

1. Taken from Victor Lee and Jerry Pipes, *Family to Family* (*Atlanta: North American Mission Board, 1999), 5.*

2. Thom Rainer and Eric Geiger, Simple Church (Nashville, TN: Broadman and Holman, 2006), and Mark Joyner, Simpleology (Hoboken, NJ: John Wiley, 2007).

3. For more on this concept in particular as it relates to students see Alvin L. Reid, Join the Movement: God Is Calling You to Change the World (Grand Rapids, MI: Kregel, 2007).

4. George Barna, Real Teens (Ventura, CA: Regal Books, 2001), 113. Barna's found about 1/3 of white and Hispanic teens and about 2/5 of African-American teens do not plan to be in church once they are independent of their parents.

5. Portions of this section were adapted from Alvin L. Reid, Raising the Bar: Ministry to Students in the New Millennium (Grand Rapids: Kregel, 2004).

6. "Personal Time Management Guide" www.time-management-guide.com/goal-time-quotes.html (2 April 2009).

7. Ibid.

Chapter 5

1. Ronald Reagan, *Public Papers of the President, Ronald Reagan, 1983, Book 1*, www.presidency.ucsb.edu/ws/index.php?pid=40728 (13 April 2009).

2. Tom Carter, ed., *2,200 Quotations From the Writings of Charles Haddon Spurgeon* (Grand Rapids, Michigan: Baker Books, 1998), 365.

3. Christina K., *Leading a Worldview Study: The Experiences of One College Student (Summit Ministries: Resources: Truth & Consequences Archives, July 2007)* www.summit.org/resources/tc/2007/07/leading-a-worldview-study.php (3 April 2009).

4. Josh McDowell and Dave Bellis, *Beyond Belief: Partnering With the Church to Rebuild the Foundations of the Faith Within This Generation* (Wheaton, IL: Tyndale, 2002), 4.

5. For an overview of the Bible's manuscripts in comparison with other ancient texts, see Alex McFarland, *The Ten Most Common Objections to Christianity* (Ventura, California: Regal Books, 2007).

6. *Sir Frederick Kenyon, Our Bible and the Ancient Manuscripts, 4th Edition* (New York: Harper and Row, 1958), 55.

7. Norman L. Geisler and Frank Turek, *I Don't Have Enough Faith to Be an Atheist (Wheaten, IL: Good News Publishers, 2004), 228.*

8. Nelson Glueck, *Rivers in the Desert: History of Negev (New York: Farrar, Straus & Cadahy, 1959), 31.*

9. William F. Albright, *Archaeology and the Religions of Israel* (Baltimore: The Johns Hopkins University Press, 1968), 176.

10. Josh McDowell, *Evidence for Christianity: Historical Evidences for the Christian Faith (Nashville: Thomas Nelson, 2006), 193.*

11. Several different internet sites contain various versions of this calculation by George Heron.

12. Colin Hemer, *The Book of Acts in the Setting of Hellenistic History (Winona Lake, IN: Eisenbrauns, 1990).*

13. For a good book on Bible study see Howard G. Hendricks and William D. Hendricks, *Living by the Book (Chicago: Moody Press, 1993).*

14. Norman L. Geisler, *Inerrancy (Grand Rapids, MI: Zondervan, 1980), 118.*

15. An excellent resource for handing difficult passages is Norman Geisler and Thomas Howe, *When Critics Ask (Grand Rapids: Baker Books, 1992).*

16. Ron Rhodes, *Esotericism and Biblical Interpretation* (Reasoning from the Scriptures) home.earthlink.net/~ronrhodes/ Esotericism.html (14 April 2009)

17. E. Harrison, ed., *Baker's Dictionary of Theology* (Grand Rapids: Baker Book House, 1960)

18. W. M. H. Paterson, L. Fuerringer, and C. O. Hofmann, comp. by George O. Lillegard, *Biblical Hermeneutics* www.wlsessays. net/files/LillegardHermeneutics.pdf (18 April 2009)

19. Geisler, *Inerrancy, 500.*

20. For a helpful overview of the Bible which clearly shows the unit of the Bible's message, see Norman L. Geisler, *To Understand the Bible Look for Jesus (Chicago: Moody Press, 1975).*

Chapter 6

None

Chapter 7

1. Jennifer Griffin-Wiesner, *Generators: 20 Activities to Recharge Your Intergenerational Group (Minneapolis, MN: Search Institute, 2005)*

2. *Angie Clark, Intergenerational Ministry* docs.wnop.org/ console/images-kids_prayer/inter_generational_ministry_ notes_dallas.pdf (7 April 2009).

3. T. Scott Daniels, "Don't Fall Into the Gap," *Holiness Today,* January/February 2007.

4. *Richard R. Dunn and Mark H. Senter III, Reaching a Generation for Christ (Chicago: Moody Press, 1997), 485*

5. *For a fascinating read on the subject of aging, read "Real Age: Are You as Young As You Can Be"* by Michael F. Roizen, M.D. and Elizabeth Anne Stephenson. You may be younger than you are OR sadly, you may be older than you really are. This book has nothing to do with your spirituality but everything to do with your physical health.

6. "Elsewhere around the country, school administrators, police, and teachers are seeing a growing tendency for girls to settle disputes through violence. They are breaking up fights in which girls are going toe-to-toe and nose-to-nose, just like the boys. Most experts contend that this trend simply is a reflection of society. In other words, girls are more violent because society in general is more violent and less civil. These experts say the

same breakdowns blamed for violence among boys are finally catching up to girls...Authorities say this is symptomatic of a disturbing trend around the county: Girls are turning to violence often and with terrifying intensity. 'We're seeing girls doing things now that we used to put off on boys,' former Baltimore school Police Chief Jansen Robinson said." Steve Vandegriff and Lee Vukich, *Disturbing Behavior: 53 Alarming Trends of Teens and How to Spot Them*, by (Chattanooga, TN: Living Ink Book, 2005), 47-48.

7. Aaron Kipnis, Angry Young Men (San Francisco: Jossey-Bass, 2002), 229.

Chapter 8

1. Several different versions of this quotation by Mark Twain are found on various internet sites.

Chapter 9

None

Chapter 10

1. George Barna, *Third Millennium Teens* (Ventura, CA: Barna Research Group, 1999), 57.

Chapter 11

1. Mike Calhoun and Mel Walker, *Pushing the Limits: Unleashing the Potential of Student Ministry* (Nashville: Thomas Nelson, 2006), 40.

Chapter 12

1. Roger Peterson, "What's Happening in Short-term Mission?" *Lausanne World Pulse.com* www.lausanneworldpulse.com/ perspectives/265/03-2006?pg=2 (18 April 2009).

2. G. Jeffrey Mac Donald, "On a mission – a short-term mission" USA Today www.usatoday.com/news/religion/2006-06-18-mission-vacations_x.htm (18 April 2009).

3. Seth Barnes, "Are short-term missions becoming faddish?" *Radical Living in a Comfortable World* www.sethbarnes. com/index.asp?filename=are-shortterm-missions-becoming-faddish (19 April 2009).

4. Jim Cottrill, "So you're the one spearheading that next mission trip. Nervous?" *Money Missions* www.moneymissions.com/jim-cottrill/short-term-missions/spearheading-a-mission-trip/ (19 April 2009).

5. Questions come from Shadow Mountain Community Church, El Cajon, CA; High School ministry, The Gathering, 2005.

6. For more details see wilderdom.com/games/descriptions/WorldMeal.html (20 April 2009).

7. Sandy Smith, curriculum writer SPLICE program of MK training, Missionary Training International, Palmer Lake, CO.

8. International Mission Board, "Moving On exercise," *Students On Mission* thetask.org/students/Approved/debriefing.htm (20 April 2009).

9. Seth Barnes, "Debriefing: #7 – Different ways to debrief" *Radical Living in a Comfortable World* www.sethbarnes.com/index.asp?filename=debriefing-7-different-ways-to-debrief (20 April 2009).

10. Seth Barnes, "Debriefing (part 5 – 30 questions to ask)" *Radical Living in a Comfortable World* www.sethbarnes.com/index.asp?filename=debriefing-part-5-30-questions-to-ask (20 April 2009).

11. International Mission Board, "Settling Back In exercise," *Students On Mission* thetask.org/students/Approved/debriefing.htm (20 April 2009).

Chapter 13

1. Richard R. Dunn and Mark H. Senter, *Reaching a Generation for Christ* (Chicago: Moody Press, 1997), 158.

2. Conversation with Dann Spader.

3. Doug Fields, *Purpose Driven Youth Ministry*, (Grand Rapids, MI: Zondervan, 1998), 369-371.

Chapter 14

1. 2001 World Christian Trends, William Carey Library, David Barrett et. al.

2. Samuel Wilson and John Siewert, eds., Mission Handbook, 13th ed. (Monrovia, California: MARC, 1986), 79-80.

3. David A. Livermore, *Serving with Eyes Wide Open: Doing Short-Term Missions with Cultural Intelligence (Grand Rapids: Baker Books, 2006), 41-42.*

4. Woodrow Kroll, The Vanishing Ministry (Grand Rapids: Kregel Publications, 2002), 14.

Chapter 15

1. *USA Today* (8/7/2007) www.usatoday.com/news/religion/2007-08-06-church-dropouts_N.htm (23 April 2009).

2. Ed Stetzer, *Lost And Found* (Nashville, TN: BH Publishing, 2009)

3. George Barna *Third-Millennium Teens* (Ventura, CA: Regal, 2001), 123.

4. Thom Rainer and Sam Rainer III, *Essential Church* (Nashville, TN: BH Publishing, 2008), 2, 15.

5. *USA Today* (8/7/2007) www.usatoday.com/news/religion/2007-08-06-church-dropouts_N.htm (23 April 2009).

6. Barna Group, "*Most Twentysomethings Put Christianity on the Self Following Spiritually Active Teen Years*" www.barna.org/barna-update/article/16-teensnext-gen/147-most-twentysomethings-put-christianity-on-the-shelf-following-spiritually-active-teen-years (26 April 2009).

7. Summit Ministries, "The Importance of Worldview Training," *Truth&Conquences*, (March, 2004) www.summit.org/resources/tc/archive/0404/ (30 April 2009)

8. Quote by Dr. Chap Clark, *National Youth Ministries Conference*, Sawmill Creek in Sandusky, OH, January 2006.

9. Gordon MacDonald, *Who Stole My Church?* (Nashville, TN: Thomas Nelson, 2007), viii.

10. Robert Laurent, *Keeping Your Teen in Touch with God* (Elgin, IL: David C. Cook, 1988), 15.

11. Steve Wright, *ReThink* (Wake Forest, NC: InQuest Ministries, 2007) 31.

12. Gary McIntosh, *One Church; Four Generations* (Grand Rapids, MI: Baker Books, 2002) 221.

13. See Mel Walker, *Mentoring the Next Generation: A Strategy for Connecting the Generations,* published by Regular Baptist Press, 2003.

Chapter 16

1. Jeffrey Brown, *The Competitive Edge (Carol Stream, IL: Tyndale House, 2007)*

2. *Jim Collins, Good to Great (New York: HarperCollins, 2001), 17-41.*

3. *Doris Kearns Goodwin, A Team of Rivals (New York: Simon & Schuster, 2005), xix.*

CONTRIBUTING WRITERS

Tim Ahlgrim
National Director
Vision For Youth, Inc.
Lafayette, Indiana
www.vfyouth.org

Glenn Amos
Special Assistant for Enrollment Services
Baptist Bible College
Clarks Summit, Pennsylvania
www.bbc.edu
gamos@bbc.edu

Mike Calhoun
Vice President
Word of Life Local Church Ministries
Schroon Lake, New York
www.wol.org

Kristen Carr
Girl's Ministry Director
First Baptist Church Atlanta
Atlanta, Georgia
www.kristencarr.com

Calvin Carr
Pastor
North Central Baptist Church
Gainesville, Florida
www.northcentralbaptist.org

Dr. Cheryl Fawcett
Vision For Youth International
Association of Baptists for World Evangelism
El Cajon, California
cfawcett@abwe.cc
www.fawcett.abwe.org

Ric Garland
Vice President
Word of Life Bible Institute
Schroon Lake, New York
www.wol.org

Ed Lewis
Executive Director
CE National, Inc.
Church Effectiveness Ministries
Winona Lake, Indiana
www.cenational.org

Dr. Alex McFarland
President
Southern Evangelical Seminary
Charlotte, North Carolina
www.alexmcfarland.com
www.ses.edu

Tom Phillips
Vice President
Word of Life Florida Ministries
Hudson, Florida
www.wol.org

Dr. Alvin Reid
Professor of Evangelism & Student Ministry
Southeastern Baptist Theological Seminary
Wake Forest, North Carolina
www.alvinreid.com
www.sebts.edu

Ken Rudolph
Director of Advancement
Lake Ann Camp
Lake Ann, Michigan
www.lakeanncamp.com

Greg Stier
President
Dare 2 Share Ministries
Arvada, Colorado
www.gregstier.org
www.dare2share.org

Dr. Jay Strack
President
Student Leadership University
Orlando, Florida
www.studentleadership.net

Dr. Steve Vandegriff
Executive Director, Center for Youth Ministries
Professor, Youth Ministries
Chair, Center for Church Ministries
Liberty University
Lynchburg, Virginia
www.liberty.edu

Mel Walker
President
Vision For Youth, Inc.
Clarks Summit, Pennsylvania
www.vfyouth.org

ABOUT THE EDITORS

MIKE CALHOUN

Vice President | Local Church Ministries

As a dynamic and articulate communicator, Mike speaks to thousands of students, leaders, and youth pastors through a diversified ministry of camps, conferences and evangelistic events. He has a deep burden for evangelism, discipleship, and development of future leadership.

In addition to *The Greenhouse Project*, Mike is the author of *Pushing the Limits: Unleashing the Potential of Student Ministry* and *First Steps, The Great Adventure Begins.* He continues an ongoing writing ministry.

Mike makes his home in Schroon Lake, New York with his wife, Betsi, who has an ongoing teaching and writing ministry to ladies and teen girls. They have three grown children: Misty (with the Lord), Joshua (wife: Kim, and granddaughter, Misty Arden) and Caleb (wife: Beth).

For more from Mike Calhoun, visit: www.mikec.wol.org

MEL WALKER

President & Co-Founder | Vision for Youth

Mel is a frequent speaker (both nationally and internationally) at youth, family life, and parenting conferences. He speaks to thousands of students and youth workers each year and has organized and led several regional, statewide and national youth conferences and events.

After serving as a youth pastor in Michigan for several years, Mel then taught youth ministry courses at Faith Baptist Bible College in Ankeny, Iowa and at Baptist Bible College & Seminary in Clarks Summit, PA. He currently serves as an adjunct faculty member at Baptist Bible Seminary and Northwest Baptist Seminary in Tacoma, Washington. Mel recently wrote three books with RBP on the subjects of youth discipleship, mentoring, and evangelism; and three booklets for VFY, including a devotional strategy for students on developing Biblical convictions.

Mel & his wife, Peggy, are the parents of three grown children: Kristi (a missionary in Germany), Todd (living at home), and Travis, along with his wife, Kaci (serving as a youth pastor in Michigan.) Mel and Peggy are active in their local church, where he directed a youth ministry internship training program.

For more from Mel Walker, visit: www.vfyouth.org

Work through *The Greenhouse Project* with a group of your student leaders using the companion *Study Guide*. Perfect for your core group or student council, the study guide provides a cost effective way to activate a strategy of Enlist, Equip, Engage where it will matter the most—at the nucleus of your youth group.

The study guide contains a synopsis of each chapter to help students make application, key thoughts to help them review their own personal life, and some study questions to help you guide a group discussion.

MORE FROM MIKE CALHOUN AND MEL WALKER

Working with youth grows more challenging and more vital to our culture every day. In *Pushing the Limits,* veteran youth workers Mike Calhoun and Mel Walker have collected some of the best writing from youth pastors and leaders around the country who are doing what it takes to tap into the true potential of youth ministry. Filled with first-hand stories from the front lines, this collection of writings is passionate and engaging.

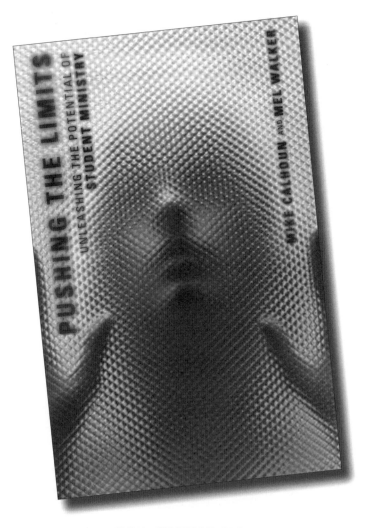